The Abominations of Modern Society

Rev. T. De. Witt Talmage

THE ABOMINATIONS OF MODERN SOCIETY.

BY REV. T. DE WITT TALMAGE,

AUTHOR OF "CRUMBS SWEPT UP"

1872.

PREFACE.

This is a buoy swung over the rocks. If it shall keep ship, bark, fore-and-aft schooner, or hermaphrodite brig from driving on a lee shore, "all's well."

The book is not more for young men than old. The Calabria was wrecked "the last day out."

Nor is the book more for men than women. The best being that God ever made is a good woman, and the worst that the devil ever made is a bad one. If anything herein shall be a warning either to man or woman, I will be glad that the manuscript was caught up between the sharp teeth of the type.

T. D.W. T.

BROOKLYN, January 1st, 1872.

CONTENTS.

The Curtain Lifted

Winter Nights

The Power of Clothes

After Midnight

The Indiscriminate Dance

The Massacre by Needle and Sewing-Machine

Pictures in the Stock Gallery

Leprous Newspapers

The Fatal Ten-Strike

Some of the Club-Houses

Flask, Bottle, and Demijohn

House of Blackness of Darkness

The Gun that Kicks over the Man who Shoots it off

Lies: White and Black

The Good Time Coming

THE CURTAIN LIFTED.

Pride of city is natural to men, in all times, if they live or have lived in a metropolis noted for dignity or prowess. Cæsar boasted of his native Rome; Lycurgus of Sparta; Virgil of Andes; Demosthenes of Athens; Archimedes of Syracuse; and Paul of Tarsus. I should suspect a man of base-heartedness who carried about with him no feeling of complacency in regard to the place of his residence; who gloried not in its arts, or arms, or behavior; who looked with no exultation upon its evidences of prosperity, its artistic embellishments, and its scientific attainments.

I have noticed that men never like a place where they have not behaved well. Swarthout did not like New York; nor Dr. Webster, Boston. Men who have free rides in prison-vans never like the city that furnishes the vehicle.

When I see in history Argos, Rhodes, Smyrna, Chios, Colophon, and several other cities claiming Homer, I conclude that Homer behaved well.

Let us not war against this pride of city, nor expect to build up ourselves by pulling others down. Let Boston have its *Common*, its *Faneuil Hall*, its *Coliseum*, and its *Atlantic Monthly*. Let Philadelphia talk about its *Mint*, and *Independence Hall*, and *Girard College*. When I find a man living in either of those places, who has nothing to say in favor of them, I feel like asking him, "What mean thing did you do, that you do not like your native city?"

New York is a goodly city. It is one city on both sides of the river. The East River is only the main artery of its great throbbing life. After a while four or five bridges will span the water, and we shall be still more emphatically one than now. When, therefore, I say "New York city, " I mean more than a million of people, including everything between Spuyten Duyvil Creek and Gowanus. That which tends to elevate a part, elevates all. That which blasts part, blasts all. Sin is a giant; and he comes to the Hudson or Connecticut River, and passes it, as easily as we step across a figure in the carpet. The blessing of God is an angel; and when it stretches out its two wings, one of them hovers over that, and the other over this.

In infancy, the great metropolis was laid down by the banks of the Hudson. Its infancy was as feeble as that of Moses, sleeping in the bulrushes by the Nile; and like Miriam, there our fathers stood and watched it. The royal spirit of American commerce came down to the water to bathe; and there she found it. She took it in her arms, and the child grew and waxed strong; and the ships of foreign lands brought gold and spices to its feet; and, stretching itself up into the proportions of a metropolis, it has looked up to the mountains, and off upon the sea, —one of the mightiest of the energies of American civilization.

The character of the founder of a city will be seen for many years in its inhabitants. Romulus impressed his life upon Rome. The Pilgrims relax not their hold upon the cities of New England. William Penn has left Philadelphia an inheritance of integrity and fair dealing; and on any day in that city you may see in the manners, customs, and principles of its people, his tastes, his coat, his hat, his wife's bonnet, and his plain meeting-house. The Hollanders still wield an influence over New York.

Grand Old New York! What southern thoroughfare was ever smitten by pestilence, when our physicians did not throw themselves upon the sacrifice! What distant land has cried out in the agony of famine, and our ships have not put out with bread-stuffs! What street of Damascus, or Beyrout, or Madras that has not heard the step of our missionaries! What struggle for national life, in which our citizens have not poured their blood into the trenches! What gallery of exquisite art, in which our painters have not hung their pictures! What department of literature or science to which our scholars have not contributed! I need not speak of our public schools, where the children of the cordwainer, and milkman, and glass-blower stand by the side of the flattered sons of millionnaires and merchant princes; or of the insane asylums on all these islands, where they who came out cutting themselves, among the tombs, now sit, clothed and in their right mind; or of the Magdalen asylums, where the lost one of the street comes to bathe the Saviour's feet with her tears, and wipe them with the hairs of her head, —confiding in the pardon of Him who said—"Let him who is without sin cast the first stone at her. " I need not speak of the institutions for the blind, the lame, the deaf and the dumb, for the incurables, for the widow, the orphan, and the outcast; or of the thousand-armed machinery that sends streaming down from the reservoir the clear, bright, sparkling, God-given water that rushes through our aqueducts, and dashes out of the hydrants, and tosses up in our fountains, and hisses in our steam-engines, and showers out the conflagration, and sprinkles from the baptismal font of our churches; and with silver note, and golden sparkle, and crystalline chime, says to hundreds of thousands of our population, in the authentic words of Him who made it—"I WILL: BE THOU CLEAN! "

They who live in any of the American cities have a goodly heritage; and it is in no depreciation of our advantages that I speak, but because, in the very contrast with our opportunities and mission, THE ABOMINATIONS are tenfold more abominable.

The sources from which I will bring the array of facts will be police, detective, and alms-house reports; city missionaries' explorations, and the testimony of the abandoned and sin-blasted, who, about to take the final plunge, have staggered back just for a moment, to utter the wild shriek of their warning, and the agonizing wail of their despair.

I shall call upon you to consider the drunkenness, the stock-gambling, the rampant dishonesties, the club-houses so far as they are nefarious, the excess of fashion, the horrors of unchastity, the bad books and unclean newspapers, and the whole range of sinful amusements; and with the plough-share of truth turn up the whole field.

If we could call up the victims themselves, they would give the most impressive story. People knew not how Turner, the painter, got such vivid conceptions of a storm at sea, until they heard the story that oftentimes he had been lashed to the deck in the midst of the tempest, in order that he might study the wrath of the sea.

Those who have themselves been tossed on the wave of infamous transgressions could give us the most vivid picture of what it is to sin and to die. With hand tremulous with exhausting disease, and hardly able to get the accursed bowl to his lips—put into such a hand the pencil, and it can sketch, as can no one else, the darkness, the fire, the wild terror, the headlong pitch, and the hell of those who have surrendered themselves to iniquity. While we dare only come near the edge, and, balancing ourselves a while, look off, and our head swims, and our breath catches, —those can tell the story best who have fallen to the depths with wilder dash than glacier from the top of a Swiss cliff, and stand, in their agony, looking up for a relief that comes not, and straining their eyes for a hope that never dawns—crying, "O God! " "O God! "

It is terrible to see a lion dashing for escape against the sides of his cage; but a more awful thing it is to behold a man, caged in bad habit, trying to break out, —blood on the soul, blood on the cage.

Others may throw garlands upon Sin, picturing the overhanging fruits which drop in her pathway, and make every step graceful as the dance; but we cannot be honest without presenting it as a giant, black with the soot of the forges where eternal chains are made, and feet rotting with disease, and breath foul with plagues, and eyes glaring with woe, and locks flowing in serpent fangs, and voice from which shall rumble forth the blasphemies of the damned.

I open to you a door, through which you see—what? Pictures and fountains, and mirrors and flowers? No: it is a lazar-house of disease. The walls drip, drip, drip with the damps of sepulchres. The victims, strewn over the floor, writhe and twist among each other in contortions indescribable, holding up their ulcerous wounds, tearing their matted hair, weeping tears of blood: some hooting with revengeful cry; some howling with a maniac's fear; some chattering with idiot's stare; some calling upon God; some calling upon fiends; wasting away; thrusting each other back; mocking each other's pains; tearing open each other's ulcers; dropping with the ichor of death! The wider I open the door, the ghastlier the scene. —Worse the horrors. More desperate recoils. Deeper curses. More blood. I can no longer endure the vision, and I shut the door, and cover my eyes, and turn my back, and cry, "God pity them! "

Some one may say, "What is the use of such an exposure as you propose to make? Our families are all respectable. " I answer, that no family, however elevated and exclusive, can be independent of the state of public morals.

However pleasant the block of houses in which you dwell, the wretchedness, the temptation, and the outrage of municipal crime will put its hand on your door-knob, and dash its awful surge against the marble of your door-steps, as the stormy sea drives on a rocky beach.

That condition of morals is now being formed, amid which our children must walk. Do you tell me it is none of my business what street profanity shall curse my boy's ear, on his way to school? Think you it is no concern of yours what infamous advertisements, placarded on the walls, or in the public newspaper, shall smite the vision of your innocent little ones? Shall I be nervous about a stagnant pool of water, lest it breed malaria, and be careless when there are in the very heart of our city thousands of houses, devoted to various forms of dissipation, which day and night steam with miasma, and pour out the fiery lava of pollution, and darken the air with their horrors, and fill the skies with the smoke of their torment, that ascendeth up forever and ever? If a slaughter-house be opened in the midst of the town, we hasten down to the Mayor to have the nuisance abated. But now I make complaint, not to the Mayor or Common Council, but to the masses of the people, who have the power to lift men up to office, and to cast them down, against a hundred thousand slaughter-houses in our American cities. In the name of our happy homes, of our refined circles, of our schools, of our churches, —in the name of all that is dear and beautiful and valuable and holy, —I enter the complaint. If you now sit unconcerned, and leave to professed philanthropists the work, and care not who are in authority or what laws remain unexecuted, you may live to see the time when you will curse the day in which your children were born.

My belief is that such an exposition of public immoralities will do good, by exciting pity for the victims and wholesale indignation against the abettors and perpetrators.

Who is that man fallen against the curbstone, covered with bruises and beastliness? He was as bright-faced a lad as ever looked up from your nursery. His mother rocked him, prayed for him, fondled him, would not let the night air touch his cheek, and held him up and looked down into his loving eyes, and wondered for what high position he was being fitted. He entered life with bright hopes. The world beckoned him, friends cheered him, but the archers shot at him; vile men set traps for him, bad habits hooked fast to him with their iron grapples; his feet slipped on the way; and there he lies. Who would think that that uncombed hair was once toyed with by a father's fingers? Who would think that those bloated cheeks were ever kissed by a mother's lips? Would you guess that that thick tongue once made a household glad with its innocent prattle? Utter no harsh words in his ear. Help him up. Put the hat over that once manly brow. Brush the dust from that coat that once covered a generous heart. Show him the way to the home that once rejoiced at the sound of his footstep, and with gentle words tell his children to stand back as you help him through the hall.

That was a kind husband once and an indulgent father. He will kneel with them no more as once he did at family prayers—the little ones with clasped hands looking up into the heavens with thanksgiving for their happy home. But now at midnight he will drive them from their pillows and curse them down the steps, and howl after them as, unclad, they fly down the street, in night-garments, under the calm starlight.

Who slew that man? Who blasted that home? Who plunged those children into worse than orphanage—until the hands are blue with cold, and the cheeks are blanched with fear, and the brow is scarred with bruises, and the eyes are hollow with grief? Who made that life a wreck, and filled eternity with the uproar of a doomed spirit?

There are those whose regular business it is to work this death. They mix a cup that glows and flashes and foams with enchantment. They call it Cognac, or Hock, or Heidsick, or Schnapps, or Old Bourbon, or Brandy, or Champagne; but they tell not that in the ruddy glow there is the blood of sacrifice, and in its flash the eye of uncoiled adders, and in the foam the mouth-froth of eternal death. Not knowing what a horrible mixture it is, men take it up and drink it down—the sacrificial blood, the adder's venom, the death-froth—and smack their lips and call it a delightful beverage.

Oh! if I had some art by which I could break the charm of the tempter's bowl, and with mailed hand lift out the long serpent of eternal despair, and shake out its coils, and cast it down, and crush it to death!

But the enchantment cannot thus be broken. It hides in the bottom of the bowl; and not until a man is entirely fallen does the monster lift itself up, and strike with its terrific fangs, and answer all his implorations for mercy with fiendish hiss. We must arouse public opinion, until city, State, and national officials shall no longer dare to neglect the execution of the law. We have enough enactments now to revolutionize our cities and strike terror through the drinking-houses and gambling-dens and houses of sin. Tracts distributed will not do it; Bibles printed will not accomplish it; city missionaries have not power for the work.

Will tracts do it? As well try with three or four snow-flakes to put out Cotapaxi!

We want police officers, common councilmen, aldermen, sheriffs, mayors, who will execute the law. Give us for two weeks in our cities an honest city hall, and public pollution would fall like lightning from heaven!

If you republicans, and you democrats, do not do your duty in this regard, we will, after a while, form a party of our own, and put men in position pledged to anti-rum, anti-dirt, anti-nuisances, anti-monopolies, anti-abominations, and will give to those of you who have been so long feeding on public spoils, careless of public morals, not so much as the wages of a street sweeper.

We are not discouraged. It may seem to many that all of our battling against these evils will come to naught. But if the coral insects can lift an island, our feeble efforts, under God, may raise a break-water that will dash back the surges of municipal abomination. Beside, we toil not in our own strength.

It seemed insignificant for Moses to stretch his hand over the Red Sea. What power could that have over the waters? But the east wind blew all night; the waters gathered into two glittering palisades on either side. The billows reared as God's hand pulled back upon their crystal bits. Wheel into line, O Israel! March! March! Pearls crash under the feet. The flying spray springs a rainbow arch over the victors. The shout of hosts mounting the beach answers the shout of hosts mid-sea; until, as the last line of the Israelites have gained the beach, the shields clang, and the cymbals clap; and as the waters whelm the pursuing foe, the swift-fingered winds on the white keys of the foam play the grand march of Israel delivered, and the awful dirge of Egyptian overthrow.

So we go forth; and stretch out the hand of prayer and Christian effort over these dark, boiling waters of crime and suffering. "Aha! Aha! " say the deriding world. But wait. The winds of divine help will begin to blow; the way will clear for the great army of Christian philanthropists; the glittering treasures of the world's beneficence will line the path of our feet; and to the other shore we will be greeted with the clash of all heaven's cymbals; while those who resist and deride and pursue us will fall under the sea, and there will be nothing left of them but here and there, cast high and dry upon the beach, the splintered wheel of a chariot, and, thrust out from the surf, the breathless nostril of a riderless charger.

WINTER NIGHTS.

The inhabitants of one of the old cities were told that they would have to fly for their lives. Such flight would be painful, even in the flush of spring-time, but superlatively aggravating if in cold weather; and therefore they were told to pray that their flight be not in the winter.

There is something in the winter season that not only tests our physical endurance, but, especially in the city, tries our moral character. It is the winter months that ruin, morally, and forever, many of our young men. We sit in the house on a winter's night, and hear the storm raging on the outside, and imagine the helpless crafts driven on the coast; but if our ears were only good enough, we could, on any winter night, hear the crash of a hundred moral shipwrecks.

Many who came last September to town, by the first of March will have been blasted. It only takes one winter to ruin a young man. When the long winter evenings have come, many of our young men will improve them in forming a more intimate acquaintance with books, contracting higher social friendships, and strengthening and ennobling their characters. But not so with all. I will show you before I get through that, at this season of the year, temptations are especially rampant: and my counsel is, *Look out how you spend your winter nights!*

I remark, first, that there is no season of the year in which vicious allurements are so active.

In warm weather, places of dissipation win their tamest triumphs. People do not feel like going, in the hot nights of summer, among the blazing gas-lights, or breathing the fetid air of assemblages. The receipts of the grog-shops in a December night are three times what they are in any night in July or August. I doubt not there are larger audiences in the casinos in winter than in the summer weather. Iniquity plies a more profitable trade. December, January, and February are harvest-months for the devil. The play-bills of the low entertainments then are more charming, the acting is more exquisite, the enthusiasm of the spectators more bewitching. Many a young man who makes out to keep right the rest of the year, capsizes now. When he came to town in the autumn, his eye was bright, his cheek rosy, his step elastic; but, before spring, as you pass him you will say to your friend, "What is the matter with that young man? " The fact is that one winter of dissipation has done the work of ruin.

This is the season for parties; and, if they are of the right kind, our social nature is improved, and our spirits cheered up. But many of them are not of the right kind; and our young people, night after night, are kept in the whirl of unhealthy excitement until their strength fails, and their spirits are broken down, and their taste for ordinary life corrupted; and, by the time the spring weather comes, they are in the doctor's hands, or sleeping in the cemetery. The certificate of their death is made out, and the physician, out of regard for the family, calls the disease by some Latin name, when the truth is that they died of too many parties.

Away with these wine-drinking convivialities! How dare you, the father of a household, trifle with the appetites of our young people? Perhaps, out of regard for the minister, or some other weak temperance man, you have the decanter in a side-room, where, after refreshments, only a select few are invited; and you come back with a glare in your eye, and a stench in your breath, that shows that you have been out serving the devil.

Some one asks, "For what purpose are these people gone into that side-room? "

"O, " replies one who has just come out, smacking his lips, "they have gone in to see the white dog! "

The excuse which Christian men often give for this is, that it is necessary, after such late eating, by some sort of stimulant to help digestion. My plain opinion is, that if a man have no more control over his appetite than to stuff himself until his digestive organs refuse to do their office, he ought not to call himself a man, but rather to class himself among the beasts that perish. I take the words of the Lord Almighty, and cry, "Woe to him that putteth the bottle to his neighbor's lips! "

Young man, take it as the counsel of a friend, when I bid you *be cautious where you spend your winter evenings*. Thank God that you have lived to see the glad winter days in which your childhood was made cheerful by the faces of fathers and mothers, brothers and sisters, some of whom, alas! will never again wish you a "happy New Year, " or a "Merry Christmas. "

Let no one tempt you out of your sobriety. I have seen respectable young men of the best families drunk on New Year's day. The excuse they gave for the inebriation was that the *ladies* insisted on their taking it. There have been instances where the delicate hand of woman hath kindled a young man's taste for strong drink, who after many years, when the attractions of that holiday scene were all forgotten, crouched in her rags, and her desolation, and her woe under the uplifted hand of the drunken monster who, on that Christmas morning so long ago, took the glass from her hand. And so, the woman stands on the abutment of the bridge, on the moon-lit night, wondering if, down under the water, there is not some quiet place for a broken heart. She takes one wild leap, —and all is over!

Ah! mingle not with the harmless beverage of your festive scene this poison of adders! Mix not with the white sugar of the cup the snow of this awful leprosy! Mar not the clatter of cutlery at the holiday feast with the clank of a madman's chain!

Stop and look into the window of that pawnbroker's shop. Elegant furs. Elegant watches. Elegant scarfs. Elegant flutes. People stand with a pleased look gazing at these things; but I look in with a shudder, as though I had seen into a window of hell.

Whose elegant watch was that? It was a drunkard's watch!

Whose furs? They belonged to a drunkard's wife!

Whose flute? Whose shoes? Whose scarf? They belonged to a drunkard's child!

If I could, I would take the three brazen balls hanging at the door-way, and clang them together until they tolled the awful knell of the drunkard's soul. The pawnbroker's shop is only one eddy of the great stream of municipal drunkenness.

Stand back, young man! Take not the first step in the path that leads here. Let not the flame of strong drink ever scorch your tongue. You may tamper with these things and escape, but your influence will be wrong. Can you not make a sacrifice for the good of others?

When the good ship *London* went down, the captain was told that there was a way of escape in one of the life-boats. He said—"No; I will go down with the rest of the passengers! " All the world acknowledged that heroism.

Can you not deny yourself insignificant indulgences for the good of others? Be not allured by the fact that you drink only the moderate beverages. You take only ale; and a man has to drink a large amount of it to become intoxicated. Yes; but there is not in all the city to-day an inebriate that did not *begin* with ale.

"XXX: " What does that mark mean? XXX on the beer-barrel: XXX on the brewer's dray: XXX on the door of the gin-shop: XXX on the side of the bottle. Not being able to find any one who could tell me what this mark means, I have had to guess that the whole thing was an allegory: XXX—that is, thirty heartbreaks. Thirty agonies. Thirty desolated homes. Thirty chances for a drunkard's grave. Thirty ways to perdition.

"XXX. " If I were going to write a story, the first chapter would be XXX. ; the last—"A pawnbroker's shop. "

Be watchful! At this season all the allurements to dissipation will be especially busy. Let not your flight to hell be in the winter.

I also remark that the winter evenings, through their very length, allow great swing for indulgences. Few young men would have the taste to go to their room at seven o'clock, and sit until eleven, reading *Motley's Dutch Republic* or *John Foster's Essays*. The young men who have been confined to the store all day want fresh air and sight-seeing; and they must go somewhere. The most of them have, of a winter's evening, three or four hours of leisure. After the evening repast, the young man puts on his hat and coat and goes out.

"Come in here, " cries one form of allurement.

"Come in here, " cries another.

"Go; " says Satan. "You ought to see for yourself. "

"Why don't you go? " says a comrade. "It is a shame for a young man to be as *green* as you are. By this time you ought to have seen everything. "

Especially is temptation strong in such times as this, when business is dull. I have noticed that men spend more money when they have little to spend.

The tremendous question to be settled by our great populace, day by day, is how to get a livelihood. Many of our young men, just starting for themselves, are very much discouraged. They had hoped before this to have set up a household of their own. But their gains have been slow, and their discouragements many. The young man can hardly take care of himself. How can he take care of another? And, to the curse of modern society, before a young man is able to set up a home of his own, he is expected to have enough to support in idleness somebody else; when God intended that they should begin together, and jointly earn a livelihood. So, many of our young men are utterly discouraged, and utterly unfit to resist temptation.

The time the pirate bears down upon the ship is when its sails are down and it is making no headway.

People wish they had more time to think. The trouble is now, that people have too much time to think. Give to many of our commercial men the four hours of these winter nights, with nothing to divert them, and before spring they will have lodgings in an insane asylum.

I remark further, that the winter is especially trying to the moral character of our young men, because some of their homes in winter are especially unattractive. In summer they can sit on the steps, or have a bouquet in the vase on the mantel; and the evenings are so short that soon after gas-light they feel like retiring. Parents do not take enough pains to make these long winter nights attractive.

It is strange that old people know so little about young people. One would think that they had never been young themselves, but had been born with their spectacles on. It is dolorous for young people to spend the three or four hours of a winter's evening with parents who sit talking over their own ailments and misfortunes, and the nothingness of this world. How dare you talk such blasphemy? God was busy six days in making the world, and has allowed it to hang six thousand years on his holy heart; and that world hath fed you, and clothed you, and shone on you for fifty years: and yet you talk about the nothingness of this world! Do you expect the young people in your family to sit a whole evening and hear you groan about this magnificent, star-lighted, sun-warmed, shower-baptized, flower-strewn, angel-watched, God-inhabited planet? From such homes young men make a wild plunge into dissipation. Many of you have the means: why do you not buy them a violin or a picture? or have your daughter cultured in music until she can help to make home attractive?

There are ten thousand ways of lighting up the domestic circle. It requires no large income, no big house, no rich wardrobe, no chased silver, no gorgeous upholstery, but a parental heart awake to its duty.

Have a doleful home and your children will not stay in it, though you block up the door with Bibles, and tie fast to them a million Heidelberg catechisms.

I said to a man, "This is a beautiful tree in front of your house. "

He answered, with a whine, "Yes; but it will fade. "

I said to him, "You have a beautiful garden. "

He replied, "Yes; but it will perish. "

I found out afterward that his son was a vagabond, and I was not surprised at it.

You cannot groan men into decency, but you can groan them out.

Pray ye that your flight be not in the winter! Devote these December, January and February evenings to high pursuits, innocent amusements, intelligent socialities, and Christian attainments. Do not waste this winter. We shall soon have seen the last snow-shower, and have passed up into the companionship of Him whose raiment is exceeding white as snow — as no fuller on earth can whiten it.

To the right-hearted, the winter nights of earth will soon end in the June morning of heaven.

The River of God, from under the Throne, never freezes over. The foliage of Life's fair tree is never frost-bitten. The festivals, and hilarities, and family gatherings of Christmas times on earth, will give way to the larger reunions, and the brighter lights, and the gladder scenes, and the sweeter garlands, and the richer feastings of the great holiday of Heaven.

THE POWER OF CLOTHES.

One cannot always tell by a man's coat what kind of a heart he has under it; still, his dress is apt to be the out-blossoming of his character, and is not to be disregarded.

We make no indiscriminate onslaught upon customs of dress. Why did God put spots on the pansy, or etch the fern leaf? And what are china-asters good for if style and color are of no importance?

The realm is as wide as the world, and as far-reaching as all the generations, over which fashion hath extended her sceptre. For thousands of years she hath sat queen over all the earth, and the revolutions that rock down all other thrones have not in the slighest affected her domination. Other constitutions have been torn, and other laws trampled; but to her decrees conquerors have bowed their plumes, and kings have uncovered. Victoria is not Queen of England; Napoleon was not Emperor of France; Isabella was not Queen of Spain. *Fashion* has been regnant over all the earth; and lords and dukes, kings and queens, have been the subjects of her realm.

She arranged the mantle of the patriarch, and the toga of the Roman; the small shoe of the Chinese women, and the turban of the Turk; the furs of the Laplander, and the calumet of the Indian chieftain. Hottentot and Siberian obey the mandate, as well as Englishman and American. Her laws are written on parchment and palm-leaf, on broken arch and cathedral tracery. She arranged how the Egyptian mummy should be wound, and how Cæsar should ride, and how the Athenians should speak, and how through the Venetian canals the gondoliers should row their pleasure-boat. Her hand hath hung the pillars with embroidery, and strewn the floor with plush. Her loom hath woven fabrics graceful as the snow and pure as the light. Her voice is heard in the gold mart, in the roar of the street, in the shuffle of the crowded bazaars, in the rattle of the steam-presses, and in the songs of the churches.

You have limited your observation of the sway of fashion if you have considered it only as it decides individual and national costumes. It makes the rules of behavior. It wields an influence in artistic spheres—often deciding what pictures shall hang in the house, what music shall be played, what ornaments shall stand upon the mantle.

The poor man will not have on his wall the cheap wood-cut that he can afford, because he cannot have a great daub like that which hangs on the rich man's wall, and costing three hundred dollars.

Fashion helps to make up religious belief. It often decides to what church we shall go, and what religious tenets we shall adopt. It goes into the pulpit, and decides the gown, and the surplice, and the style of rhetoric.

It goes into literature and arranges the binding, the type, the illustrations of the book, and oftentimes the sentiments expressed and the theories evolved.

Men the most independent in feeling are by it compelled to submit to social customs. And before I stop I want to show you that fashion has been one of the most potent of reformers, and one of the vilest of usurpers. Sometimes it has been an angel from heaven, and at others it has been the mother of harlots.

As the world grows better there will be as much fashion as now, but it will be a different fashion. In the future life white robes always have been and always will be in the fashion.

There is a great outcry against this submission to social custom, as though any consultation of the tastes and feelings of others were deplorable; but without it the world would have neither law, order, civilization, nor common decency.

There has been a canonization of bluntness. There are men and women who boast that they can tell you all they know and hear about you, especially if it be unpleasant. Some have mistaken rough behavior for frankness, when the two qualities do not belong to the same family. You have no right, with your eccentricities, to crash in upon the sensitiveness of others. There is no virtue in walking with hoofs over fine carpets. The most jagged rock is covered with blossoming moss. The storm that comes jarring down in thunder strews rainbow colors upon the sky, and silvery drops on orchard and meadow.

There are men who pride themselves on their capacity to "stick" others. They say "I have brought him down: Didn't I make him squirm! "

Others pride themselves on their outlandish apparel. They boast of being out of the fashion. They wear a queer hat. They ride in an odd carriage. By dint of perpetual application they would persuade the world that they are perfectly indifferent to public opinion. They are more proud of being "out of fashion" than others are of being in. They are utterly and universally disagreeable. Their rough corners have never been worn off. They prefer a hedge-hog to a lamb.

The accomplishments of life are in nowise productive of effeminacy or enervation. Good manners and a respect for the tastes of others is indispensable. The Good Book speaks favorably of those who are a *"peculiar"* people; but that does not sanction the behavior of *queer* people. There is no excuse, under any circumstances, for not being and acting the lady or gentleman. Rudeness is sin. We have no words too ardent to express our admiration for the refinements of society. There is no law, moral or divine, to forbid elegance of demeanor, ornaments of gold or gems for the person, artistic display in the dwelling, gracefulness of gait and bearing, polite salutation, or honest compliments; and he who is shocked or offended by these had better, like the old Scythians, wear tiger-skins, and take one wild leap back into midnight barbarism.

As Christianity advances there will be better apparel, higher styles of architecture, more exquisite adornments, sweeter music, grander pictures, more correct behavior, and more thorough ladies and gentlemen.

But there is another story to be told. Excessive fashion is to be charged with many of the worst evils of society, and its path has often been strewn with the bodies of the slain.

It has often set up a false standard by which people are to be judged. Our common sense, as well as all the divine intimations on the subject, teach us that people ought to be esteemed according to their individual and moral attainments. The man who has the most nobility of soul should be first, and he who has the least of such qualities should stand last. No crest, or shield, or escutcheon, can indicate one's moral peerage. Titles of duke, lord, esquire, earl, viscount, or patrician, ought not to raise one into the first rank. Some of the meanest men I have ever known had at the end of their name D. D., LL. D., and F. R.S. Truth, honor, charity, heroism, self-sacrifice, should win highest favor; but inordinate fashion says—"Count not a woman's virtues; count her rings; " "Look not at the contour of the head, but see the way she combs her hair; " "Ask not what noble deeds have been accomplished by that man's hand; but is it white and soft? " Ask not what good sense was in her conversation, but "in what was she dressed. " Ask not whether there was hospitality and cheerfulness in the house, but "in what style do they live. "

As a consequence, some of the most ignorant and vicious men are at the top, and some of the most virtuous and intelligent at the bottom. During the late war we suddenly saw men hurled up into the highest social positions. Had they suddenly reformed from evil habits? or graduated in a science? or achieved some good work for society? No! They simply had obtained a government contract!

This accounts for the utter chagrin which men feel at the treatment they receive when they lose their property. Hold up your head amid financial disaster, like a Christian! Fifty thousand subtracted from a good man leaves how much? Honor; Truth; Faith in God; Triumphant Hope; and a kingdom of ineffable glory, over which he is to reign forever and ever.

If a millionnaire should lose a penny out of his pocket, would he sit down on a curb-stone and cry? And shall a man possessed of everlasting fortunes wear himself out with grief because he has lost worldly treasure? You have only lost that in which hundreds of wretched misers surpass you; and you have saved that which the Cæsars, and the Pharaohs, and the Alexanders could never afford.

And yet society thinks differently; and you see the most intimate friendships broken up as the consequence of financial embarrassments. You say to some one — "How is your friend — —? " The man looks bewildered, and says, "I do not know. " You reply, "Why; you used to be intimate. " "Well, " says the man, "our friendship has been dropped: the man has failed. "

Proclamation has gone forth: "Velvets must go up, and homespun must come down; " and the question is "How does the coat fit? " — not, "Who wears it? " The power that bears the tides of excited population up and down our streets, and rocks the world of commerce, and thrills all nations, Transatlantic and Cisatlantic, is — *clothes*. It decides the last offices of respect; and how long the dress shall be totally black; and when it may subside into spots of grief on silk, calico, or gingham. Men die in good circumstances, but by reason of extravagant funeral expenses are well nigh insolvent before they get buried. Many men would not die at all, if they had to wait until they could afford it.

Excessive fashion is productive of a most ruinous strife. The expenditure of many households is adjusted by what their neighbors have, not by what they themselves can afford to have; and the great anxiety is as to who shall have the finest house and the most costly equipage. The weapons used in the warfare of social life are not Minié rifles, and Dahlgren guns, and Hotchkiss shells, but chairs and mirrors, and vases, and Gobelins, and Axminsters. Many household establishments are like racing steamboats, propelled at the utmost strain and risk, and just coming to a terrific explosion. "Who cares, " say they, "if we only come out ahead? "

There is no one cause to-day of more financial embarrassment, and of more dishonesties, than this determination, at all hazards, to live as well as or better than other people. There are persons who will risk their eternity upon one fine looking-glass, or who will dash out the splendors of heaven to get another trinket.

"My house is too small. " "But, " says some one, "you cannot pay for a larger. " "Never mind that; my friends have a better residence, and so will I. " "A dress of that pattern I must have. I cannot afford it by a great deal; but who cares for that? My neighbor had one from that pattern, and I must have one. " There are scores of men in the dungeons of the penitentiary, who risked honor, business, — everything, in the effort to shine like others. Though the heavens fall, they must be "in the fashion. "

The most famous frauds of the day have resulted from this feeling. It keeps hundreds of men struggling for their commercial existence. The trouble is that some are caught and incarcerated, if their larceny be small. If it be great, they escape, and build their castle on the Rhine. Men go into jail, not because they steal, but because they did not steal enough.

Again: excessive fashion makes people unnatural and untrue. It is a factory from which has come forth more hollow pretences, and unmeaning flatteries, and hypocrisies, than the Lowell Mills ever turned out shawls and garments.

Fashion is the greatest of all liars. It has made society insincere. You know not what to believe. When people ask you to come, you do not know whether or not they want you to come. When they send their regards, you do not know whether it is an expression of their heart, or an external civility. We have learned to take almost everything at a discount. Word is sent, "Not at home, " when they are only too lazy to dress themselves. They say, "The furnace has just gone out, " when in truth they have had no fire in it all winter. They apologize for the unusual barrenness of their table, when they never live any better. They decry their most luxurious entertainments, to win a shower of approval. They apologize for their appearance, as though it were unusual, when always at home they look just so. They would make you believe that some nice sketch on the wall was the work of a master painter. "It was an heir-loom, and once hung on the walls of a castle; and a duke gave it to their grandfather. " People who will lie about nothing else, will lie about a picture. On a small income we must make the world believe that we are affluent, and our life becomes a cheat, a counterfeit, and a sham.

Few persons are really natural. When I say this, I do not mean to slur cultured manners. It is right that we should have more admiration for the sculptured marble than for the unhewn block of the quarry. From many circles in life fashion has driven out vivacity and enthusiasm. A frozen dignity instead floats about the room, and iceberg grinds against iceberg. You must not laugh outright: it is vulgar. You must *smile*. You must not dash rapidly across the room: you must *glide*. There is a round of bows, and grins, and flatteries, and oh's! and ah's! and simperings, and namby-pambyism—a world of which is not worth one good, round, honest peal of laughter. From such a hollow round the tortured guest retires at the close of the evening, and assures his host that he has enjoyed himself.

Thus social life has been contorted, and deformed, until, in some mountain cabin, where rustics gather to the quilting or the apple-paring, there is more good cheer than in all the frescoed ice-houses of the metropolis.

We want, in all the higher circles of society, more warmth of heart and naturalness of behavior, and not so many refrigerators.

Again: inordinate fashion is incompatible with happiness. Those who depend for their comfort upon the admiration of others are subject to frequent disappointment. Somebody will criticise their appearance, or surpass them in brilliancy, or will receive more attention. Oh! the jealousy, and detraction, and heart-burnings of those who move in this bewildered maze!

The clock strikes *one*, and the company begins to disperse. The host has done everything to make all his guests happy; but now that they are on the street, hear their criticisms of everybody and everything. "Did you see her in such and such apparel? " "Wasn't she a perfect fright! " "What a pity that such an one is so awkward and uncouth! " "Well, really, —I would rather never be spoken to than be seen with such a man as that! "

Poor butterflies! Bright wings do not always bring happiness. "She that liveth in pleasure is dead while she liveth. " The revelations of high life that come to the challenge and the fight are only the occasional croppings out of disquietudes that are, underneath, like the stars of heaven for multitude, but like the demons of the pit for hate. The misery that to-night in the cellar cuddles up in the straw is not so utter as the princely disquietude which stalks through splendid drawing-rooms, brooding over the slights and offences of high life. The bitterness of trouble seems not so unfitting, when drunk out of a pewter mug, as when it pours from the chased lips of a golden chalice. In the sharp crack of the voluptuary's pistol, putting an end to his earthly misery, I hear the confirmation that in a hollow, fastidious life there is no peace.

Again: Excessive devotion to fashion is productive of physical disease, mental imbecility, and spiritual withering.

Apparel insufficient to keep out the cold and the rain, or so fitted upon the person that the functions of life are restrained; late hours, filled with excitement and feasting; free draughts of wine, that make one not beastly intoxicated, but only fashionably drunk; and luxurious indolence—are the instruments by which this unreal life pushes its disciples into valetudinarianism and the grave. Along the walks of high life Death goes a mowing—and such harvests as are reaped! *Materia medica* has been exhausted to find curatives for these physiological devastations. Dropsies, cancers, consumptions, gout, and almost every infirmity in all the realm of pathology, have been the penalty paid. To counteract the damage, pharmacy has gone forth with medicament, panacea, elixir, embrocation, salve, and cataplasm.

To-night, with swollen feet, upon cushioned ottoman, and groaning with aches innumerable, is the votary of luxurious living, not half so happy as his groom or coal-heaver.

Fashion is the world's undertaker, and drives thousands of hearses to Laurel Hill and Greenwood.

But, worse than that, this folly is an intellectual depletion. This endless study of proprieties and etiquette, patterns and styles, is bedwarfing to the intellect. I never knew a man or a woman of extreme fashion that knew much. How belittling the study of the cut of a coat, or the tie of a cravat, or the wrinkle in a shoe, or the color of a ribbon! How they are worried if something gets untied, or hangs awry, or is not nicely adjusted! With a mind capable of measuring the height and depth of great subjects; able to unravel mysteries; to walk through the universe; to soar up into the infinity of God's attributes, —hovering perpetually over a new style of mantilla! I have known men, reckless as to their character, and regardless of interests momentous and eternal, exasperated by the shape of a vest-button!

What is the matter with that woman—wrought up into the agony of despair? O, her muff is out of fashion!

Worse than all—this folly is not satisfied until it has extirpated every moral sentiment, and blasted the soul. A wardrobe is the rock upon which many a soul has been riven. The excitement of a luxurious life has been the vortex that has swallowed up more souls than the Maelstrom off Norway ever devoured ships. What room for elevating themes in a heart filled with the trivial and unreal? Who can wonder that in this haste for sun-gilded bawbles and winged thistle-down, men should tumble into ruin? The travellers to destruction are not all clothed in rags. On that road chariot jostles against chariot; and behind steeds in harness golden-plated and glittering, they go down, coach and four, herald and postilion, racketing on the hot pavements of hell. Clear the track! Bazaars hang out their colors over the road; and trees of tropical fruitfulness overbranch the way. No sound of woe disturbs the air; but all is light and song, and wine and gorgeousness. The world comes out to greet the dazzling procession with Hurrah! and Hurrah! But, suddenly, there is a halt and an outcry of dismay, and an overthrow worse than the Red Sea tumbling upon the Egyptians. Shadow of grave-stones upon finest silk! Wormwood squeezed into impearled goblets!

Death, with one cold breath, withering the leaves and freezing the fountains.

In the wild tumult of the last day—the mountains falling, the heavens flying, the thrones uprising, the universe assembling; amid the boom of the last great thunder-peal, and under the crackling of a burning world—what will become of the fop and the dandy?

He who is genuinely refined will be useful and happy. There is no gate that a gentleman's hand cannot open. During his last sickness there will be a timid knock at the basement door by those who have come to see how he is.

But watch the career of one thoroughly artificial. Through inheritance, or perhaps his own skill, having obtained enough for purposes of display, he feels himself thoroughly established. He sits aloof from the common herd, and looks out of his window upon the poor man, and says—"Put that dirty wretch off my steps immediately! " On Sabbath days he finds the church, but mourns the fact that he must worship with so many of the inelegant, and says, "They are perfectly awful! " "That man that you put in my pew had a coat on his back that did not cost five dollars. " He struts through life unsympathetic with trouble, and says, "I cannot be bothered. " Is delighted with some doubtful story of Parisian life, but thinks that there are some very indecent things in the Bible. Walks arm in arm with a millionnaire, but does not know his own brother. Loves to be praised for his splendid house; and when told that he looks younger than ten years ago, says—"Well, really; do you think so! "

But the brief strut of his life is about over. Up-stairs—he dies. No angel wings hovering about him. No gospel promises kindling up the darkness; —but exquisite embroidery, elegant pictures, and a bust of Shakespeare on the mantel. The pulses stop. The minister comes in to read of the Resurrection, that day when the dead shall come up—both he that died on the floor, and he that expired under princely upholstery. He is carried out to burial. Only a few mourners, but a great array of carriages. Not one common man at the funeral. No befriended orphan to weep a tear upon his grave. No child of want pressing through the ranks of the weeping, saying—"He is the last friend I have; and I must see him. "

What now? He was a great man: Shall not chariots of salvation come down to the other side of the Jordan, and escort him up to the palace? Shall not the angels exclaim—"Turn out! a prince is coming." Will the bells chime? Will there be harpers with their harps, and trumpeters with their trumpets?

No! No! No! There will be a shudder, as though a calamity had happened. Standing on heaven's battlement, a watchman will see something shoot past, with fiery downfall, and shriek: "Wandering star—for whom is reserved the blackness of darkness forever! "

With the funeral pageant the brilliant career terminated. There was a great array of carriages.

AFTER MIDNIGHT.

When night came down on Babylon, Nineveh, and Jerusalem, they needed careful watching, otherwise the incendiary's torch might have been thrust into the very heart of the metropolitan splendor; or enemies, marching from the hills, might have forced the gates. All night long, on top of the wall and in front of the gates, might be heard the measured step of the watchman on his solitary beat; silence hung in air, save as some passer-by raised the question: "Watchman, what of the night? "

It is to me a deeply suggestive and solemn thing to see a man standing guard by night. It thrilled through me, as at the gate of an arsenal in Charleston, the question once smote me, "Who comes there? " followed by the sharp command: "Advance and give the countersign. " Every moral teacher stands on picket, or patrols the wall as watchman. His work is to sound the alarm; and whether it be in the first watch, in the second watch, in the third watch, or in the fourth watch, to be vigilant until the daybreak flings its "morning glories" of blooming cloud across the arching trellis of the sky.

The ancients divided their night into four parts—the first watch, from six to nine; the second, from nine to twelve; the third, from twelve to three; and the fourth, from three to six.

I speak now of the city in the third watch, or from twelve to three o'clock.

I never weary of looking upon the life and brilliancy of the city in the *first* watch. That is the hour when the stores are closing. The laboring men, having quitted the scaffolding and the shop, are on their way home. It rejoices me to give them my seat in the city car. They have stood and hammered away all day. Their feet are weary. They are exhausted with the tug of work. They are mostly cheerful. With appetites sharpened on the swift turner's wheel and the carpenter's whetstone, they seek the evening meal. The clerks, too, have broken away from the counter, and with brain weary of the long line of figures, and the whims of those who go a-shopping, seek the face of mother, or wife and child. The merchants are unharnessing themselves from their anxieties, on their way up the street. The boys that lock up are heaving away at the shutters, shoving the heavy bolts, and taking a last look at the fire to see that all is safe. The streets are thronged with young men, setting out from the great centres of bargain-making.

Let idlers clear the street, and give right of way to the besweated artisans and merchants! They have *earned* their bread, and are now on their way home to get it.

The lights in full jet hang over ten thousand evening repasts—the parents at either end of the table, the children between. Thank God! "who setteth the solitary in families! "

A few hours later, and all the places of amusement, good and bad, are in full tide. Lovers of art, catalogue in hand, stroll through the galleries and discuss the pictures. The ball-room is resplendent with the rich apparel of those who, on either side of the white, glistening boards, await the signal from the orchestra. The footlights of the theatre flash up; the bell rings, and the curtain rises; and out from the gorgeous scenery glide the actors, greeted with the vociferation of the expectant multitudes. Concert-halls are lifted into enchantment with the warble of one songstress, or swept out on a sea of tumultuous feeling by the blast of brazen instruments. Drawing-rooms are filled with all gracefulness of apparel, with all sweetness of sound, with all splendor of manner; mirrors are catching up and multiplying the scene, until it seems as if in infinite corridors there were garlanded groups advancing and retreating.

The out-door air rings with laughter, and with the moving to and fro of thousands on the great promenades. The dashing span, adrip with the foam of the long country ride, rushes past as you halt at the curb-stone.

Mirth, revelry, beauty, fashion, magnificence mingle in the great metropolitan picture, until the thinking man goes home to think more seriously, and the praying man to pray more earnestly.

A beautiful and overwhelming thing is the city in the first and second watches of the night.

But the clock strikes twelve, and the third watch begins. The thunder of the city has rolled from the air. Slight sounds now cut the night with a distinctness that excites your attention. You hear the tinkling of the bell of the street-car in the far distance; the baying of the dog; the stamp of the horse in the adjoining street; the slamming of a saloon door; the hiccoughing of the inebriate; and the shriek of the steam-whistle five miles away. Solemn and stupendous is this third watch. There are respectable men abroad. The city missionary is going up that court, to take a scuttle of coal to a poor family. The undertaker goes up the steps of that house, from which there comes a bitter cry, as though the destroying angel had smitten the first-born. The minister of Jesus passes along; he has been giving the sacrament to a dying Christian. The physician hastens past, the excited messenger a few steps ahead, impatient to reach the threshold. Men who are forced to toil into the midnight are hastening to their pillow. But the great multitudes are asleep. The lights are out in the dwellings, save here and there one. That is the light of the watcher, for the remedies must be administered, and the fever guarded, and the restless tossing of the coverlet resisted, and the ice kept upon the temples, and the perpetual prayer offered by hearts soon to be broken. The street-lamps, standing in long line, reveal the silence and the slumber of the town.

Stupendous thought: a great city asleep! Weary arm gathering strength for to-morrow's toil. Hot brain getting cooled off. Rigid muscles relaxing. Excited nerves being soothed. White locks of the octogenarian in thin drifts across the white pillow—fresh fall of flakes on snow already fallen. Children with dimpled hands thrown put over the pillow, with every breath inhaling a new store of fun and frolic.

Let the great hosts sleep! A slumberless Eye will watch them. Silent be the alarm-bells and merciful the elements! Let one great wave of refreshing slumber roll across the heart of the great town, submerging trouble and weariness and pain. It is the third watch of the night, and time for the city to sleep.

But be not deceived. There are thousands of people in the great town who will not sleep a moment to-night. Go up that dark court. Be careful, or you will fall over the prostrate form of a drunkard lying on his own worn step. Look about you, or you will feel the garroter's hug. Try to look in through that broken pane! What do you see? Nothing. But listen. What is it? "God help us! " No footlights, but tragedy—mightier, ghastlier than Ristori or Edwin Booth ever acted. No bread. No light. No fire. No cover. They lie strewn upon the floor—two whole families in one room. They shiver in the darkness. They have had no food to-day. You say: "Why don't they beg? "

They did beg, but got nothing. You say: "Hand them over to the almshouse. "

Ah! they had rather die than go to the almshouse. Have you never heard the bitter cry of the man or of the child when told that he must go to the almshouse?

You say that these are vicious poor, and have brought their own misfortune on themselves.

So much the more to be pitied. The Christian poor—God helps them! Through their night there twinkles the round, merry star of hope, and through the cracked window-pane of their hovel they see the crystals of heaven. But the vicious are the more to be pitied. They have no hope. They are in hell now. They have put out their last light. People excuse themselves from charity by saying they do not deserve to be helped. If I have ten prayers for the innocent, I shall have twenty for the guilty. If a ship be dashed upon the rocks, the fisherman, in his hut on the beach, will wrap the warmest flannels around those who are the most chilled and battered. The vicious poor have suffered two awful wrecks, the wreck of the body, and the wreck of the soul; a wreck for time and a wreck for eternity.

Go up that alley! Open the door. It is not locked. They have nothing to lose. No burglar would want anything that is there. There is only a broken chair set against the door. Strike a match and look around you. Beastliness and rags! A shock of hair hanging over the scarred visage. Eyes glaring upon you. Offer no insult. Be careful what you say. Your life is not worth much in such a place. See that red mark on the wall. That is the mark of a murderer's hand. From the corner a wild face starts out of the straw and moves toward you, just as your light goes out.

Strike another match. Here is a little babe. It does not laugh. It never will laugh. A sea-flower flung on an awfully barren beach: O that the Shepherd would fold that lamb! Wrap your shawl about you, for the January wind sweeps in. Strike another match. The face of that young woman is bruised and gashed now, but a mother once gazed upon it in ecstasy of fondness. Awful stare of two eyes that seem looking up from the bottom of woe. Stand back. No hope has dawned on that soul for years. Hope never will dawn upon it. Utter no scorn. The match has gone out. Light it not again, for it would seem to be a mockery.

Pass out! Pass on! Know that there are thousands of such abodes in our cities. An awful, gloomy, and overwhelming picture is the city in the third watch.

After midnight the crime of the city does its chief work. At eight and a half o'clock in the evening the criminals of the city are at leisure. They are mostly in the drinking saloons. It needs courage to do what they propose to do. Rum makes men reckless. They are getting their brain and hand just right. Toward midnight they go to their garrets. They gather their tools. Soon after the third watch they stalk forth, silently, looking out for the police, through the alleys to their appointed work. This is a burglar; and the door-lock will fly open at the touch of the false keys. That is an incendiary; and before morning there will be a light on the sky, and a cry of "Fire! Fire! " That is an assassin; and a lifeless body will be found to-morrow in some of the vacant lots.

During all the day there are hundreds of villains to be found lounging about, a part of the time asleep, apart of the time awake; but at twelve to-night they will rouse up, and their eyes will be keen, and their minds acute, and their arms strong, and their foot fleet to fly or pursue. Many of them have been brought up to the work. They were born in a thief's garret. Their childish plaything was a burglar's dark lantern. As long ago as they can remember, they saw, toward morning, the mother binding up the father's head, wounded by a watchman's billet. They began by picking boys' pockets, and now they can dig an underground passage to the cellar of the bank, or will blast open the door of the gold vault. So long as the children of the street are neglected there will be no lack of desperadoes.

In the third watch of the night the gambling-houses are in full blast. What though the hours of the night are slipping away, and the wife sits waiting in the cheerless home! Stir up the fires! Bring on the drinks! Put up the stakes! A whole fortune may be made before morning! Some of the firms that two years ago first put out their sign of copartnership have already foundered on the gambler's table. The money-drawer in many a mercantile house will this year mysteriously spring a leak. Gaming is a portentous vice, and is making great efforts to become respectable. Recently a member of Congress played with a member elect, carrying off a trophy of one hundred and twenty thousand dollars. The old-fashioned way of getting a fortune is too slow! Let us toss up and see who shall have it!

And so it goes, from the wheezing wretches who pitch pennies in a rum grocery, to the millionnaire gamblers in the gold-market.

After midnight the eye of God will look down and see uncounted gambling-saloons plying their destruction. Passing down the street to-night, you may hear the wrangling of the gamblers mingling with the rattle of the dice, and the clear, sharp crack of the balls on the billiard-table.

The finest rooms in the city are gambling dens. In gilded parlor, amid costly tapestry, you may behold these dens of death. These houses have walls attractive with elaborate fresco and gems of painting—no sham artist's daub, but a masterpiece. Mantel and table glitter with vases and statuettes. Divans and lounges with deep cushions, the perfection of upholstery, invite to rest and repose. Aquaria alive with fins and strewn with tinged shells and zoophytes. Tufts of geranium, from bead baskets, suspended mid-room, drop their witching perfume. Fountains gushing up, sprinkling the air with sparkles, or gushing through the mouth of the marble lion. Long mirrors, mounted with scrolls and wings and exquisite carvings, catching and reflecting back the magnificence. At their doors merchant-princes dismount from their carriages; official dignitaries enter; legislators, tired of making laws, here take a respite in breaking them.

From all classes this crime is gathering its victims: the importer of foreign silks, and the Chatham street dealer in pocket-handkerchiefs; clerks taking a game in the store after the shutters are put up; and officers of the court whiling away the time while the jury are out. In the woods around Baden Baden, in the morning, it is no rare thing to find the suspended bodies of suicides. No splendor of surroundings can hide the dreadful nature of this sin. In the third watch of this very night, the tears of thousands of orphans and widows will dash up in those fountains. The thunders of eternal destruction roll in the deep rumble of that ten-pin alley. And as from respectable circles young men and old are falling in line of procession, all the drums of woe begin to beat the dead march of ten thousand souls.

Seven millions of dollars are annually lost in New York city at the gaming-table. Some of your own friends may be at it. The agents of these gaming-houses around our hotels are well dressed. They meet a stranger in the city; they ask him if he would like to see the city; he says, "Yes; " they ask him if he has seen that splendid building up town, and he says "No. " "Then, " says the villain to the greenhorn,"I will show you the lions and the elephants. " After seeing the lions and the elephants, I would not give much for a young man's chance for decency or heaven. He looks in, and sees nothing objectionable; but let him beware, for he is on enchanted ground. Look out for the men who have such sleek hats—always sleek hats—and such a patronizing air, and who are so unaccountably interested in your welfare and entertainment. All that they want of you is your money. A young man on Chestnut street, Philadelphia, lost in a night all his money at the gaming-table, and, before he left the table, blew his brains out; but before the maid had cleaned up the blood the players were again at the table, shuffling away. A wolf has more compassion for the lamb whose blood it licks up; a highwayman more love for the belated traveller upon whose carcass he piles the stone; the frost more feeling for the flower it kills; the fire more tenderness for the tree-branch it consumes; the storm more pity for the ship that it shivers on Long Island coast, than a gambler's heart has mercy for his victim.

Deed of darkness unfit for sunlight, or early evening hour! Let it come forth only when most of the city lights are out, in the third watch of the night!

Again, it is after twelve o'clock that drunkenness shows its worst deformity! At eight or nine o'clock the low saloons are not so ghastly. At nine o'clock the victims are only talkative. At ten o'clock they are much flushed. At eleven o'clock their tongue is thick, and their hat occasionally falls from the head. At twelve they are nauseated and blasphemous, and not able to rise. At one they fall to the floor, asking for more drink. At two o'clock, unconscious and breathing hard. They would not fly though the house took fire. Soaked, imbruted, dead drunk! They are strewn all over the city, in the drinking saloons, —fathers, brothers, and sons; men as good as you, naturally—perhaps better.

Not so with the higher circles of intoxication. The "gentlemen" coax their fellow-reveller to bed, or start with him for home, one at each arm, holding him up; the night air is filled with his hooting and cursing. He will be helped into his own door. He will fall into the entry. Hush it up! Let not the children of the house be awakened to hear the shame. He is one of the merchant princes.

But you cannot always hush it up.

Drink makes men mad. One of its victims came home and found that his wife had died during his absence; and he went into the room where she had been prepared for the grave, and shook her from the shroud, and tossed her body out of the window. Where sin is loud and loathsome and frenzied, it is hard to keep it still. This whole land is soaked with the abomination. It became so bad in Massachusetts, that the State arose in indignation; and having appointed agents for the sale of alcohol for mechanical and medicinal purposes, prohibited the general traffic under a penalty of five hundred dollars. The popular proprietors of the Revere, Tremont, and Parker Houses were arrested. The grog-shops diminished in number from six thousand to six hundred. God grant that the time may speed on when all the cities and States shall rouse up, and put their foot upon this abomination.

As you pass along the streets, night by night, you will see the awful need that something radical be done. But you do not see the worst. That will come to pass long after you are sleeping—in the third watch of the night.

Oh! ye who have been longing for fields of work, here they are before you. At the London midnight meetings, thirteen thousand of the daughters of sin were reformed; and uncounted numbers of men, who were drunken and debauched, have been redeemed. If from our highest circles a few score of men and women would go forth among the wandering and the destitute, they might yet make the darkest alley of the town kindle with the gladness of heaven. Do not go in your warm furs, and from your well-laden tables, thinking that pious counsel will stop the gnawing of empty stomachs or warm their stockingless feet. Take food and medicine, and raiment, as well as a prayer. When the city missionary told the destitute woman she ought to love God, she said: "Ah! if you were as cold and hungry as I am, you could think of nothing else. "

I am glad to know that not one earnest prayer, not one heartfelt alms-giving, not one kind word, ever goes unblessed. Among the mountains of Switzerland there is a place where, if your voice be uttered, there will come back a score of echoes. But utter a kind, sympathetic, and saving word in the dark places of the town, and there will come back ten thousand echoes from all the thrones of heaven.

There may be some one reading this who knows by experience of the tragedies enacted in the third watch of the night. I am not the man to thrust you back with one harsh word. Take off the bandage from your soul, and put on it the salve of the Saviour's compassion. There is rest in God for your tired soul. Many have come back from their wanderings. I see them coming now. Cry up the news to heaven! Set all the bells a-ringing! Under the high arch spread the banquet of rejoicing. Let all the crowned heads of heaven come in and keep the jubilee. I tell you there is more joy in heaven over one man who reforms than over ninety-and-nine who never got off the track.

But there is a man who will never return from his evil ways. How many acts are there in a tragedy? Five, I believe:

ACT I. —*Young man starting from home. Parents and sisters weeping to have him go. Wagon passing over the hills. Farewell kiss thrown back. Ring the bell and let the curtain drop.*

ACT II. —*Marriage altar. Bright lights. Full organ. White veil trailing through the aisle. Prayer and congratulation, and exclamations of "How well she looks! " Ring the bell, and let the curtain drop.*

ACT III. —*Midnight. Woman waiting for staggering steps. Old garments stuck into the broken window-pane. Many marks of hardship on the face. Biting of the nails of bloodless fingers. Neglect, cruelty, disgrace. Ring the bell, and let the curtain drop.*

ACT IV. —*Three graves in a very dark place. Grave of child who died from lack of medicine. Grave of wife who died of a broken heart. Grave of husband and father who died of dissipation. Plenty of weeds, but no flowers. O what a blasted heath with three graves! Ring the bell, and let the curtain drop.*

ACT V. —*A destroyed soul's eternity. No light; no music; no hope! Despair coiling around the heart with unutterable anguish. Blackness of darkness forever.*

Woe! Woe! Woe! I cannot bear longer to look. I close my eyes at this last act of the tragedy. Quick! Quick! Ring the bell and let the curtain drop.

THE INDISCRIMINATE DANCE.

It is the anniversary of Herod's birthday. The palace is lighted. The highways leading thereto are ablaze with the pomp of invited guests. Lords, captains, merchant princes, and the mightiest men of the realm are on the way to mingle in the festivities. The tables are filled with all the luxuries that the royal purveyors can gather, —spiced wines, and fruits, and rare meats. The guests, white-robed, anointed and perfumed, take their places. Music! The jests evoke roars of laughter. Riddles are propounded. Repartees indulged. Toasts drunk. The brain befogged. Wit gives place to uproar and blasphemy. And yet they are not satisfied. Turn on more light. Give us more music. Sound the trumpet. Clear the floor for the dance. Bring in Salome, the graceful and accomplished princess.

The doors are opened and in bounds the dancer. Stand back and give plenty of room for the gyrations. The lords are enchanted. They never saw such poetry of motion. Their souls whirl in the reel, and bound with the bounding feet. Herod forgets crown and throne, — everything but the fascinations of Salome. The magnificence of his realm is as nothing compared with that which now whirls before him on tiptoe. His heart is in transport with Salome as her arms are now tossed in the air, and now placed akimbo. He sways with every motion of the enchantress. He thrills with the quick pulsations of her feet, and is bewitched with the posturing and attitudes that he never saw before, in a moment exchanged for others just as amazing. He sits in silence before the whirling, bounding, leaping, flashing wonder. And when the dance stops, and the tinkling cymbals pause, and the long, loud plaudits that shook the palace with their thunders had abated, the entranced monarch swears unto the princely performer: "Whatsoever thou shalt ask of me I will give it to thee, to the half of my kingdom. "

Now there was in prison a minister by the name of John the Baptist, who had made much trouble by his honest preaching. He had denounced the sins of the king, and brought down upon himself the wrath of the females in the royal family. At the instigation of her mother, Salome takes advantage of the king's extravagant promise and demands the head of John the Baptist on a dinner-plate.

There is a sound of heavy feet, and the clatter of swords outside of the palace. Swing back the door. The executioners are returning, from their awful errand. They hand a platter to Salome. What is that on the platter? A new tankard of wine to rekindle the mirth of the lords? No! It is redder than wine, and costlier. It is the ghastly, bleeding head of John the Baptist! Its locks dabbled in gore. Its eyes set in the death-stare. The distress of the last agony in the features. That fascinating form, that just now swayed so gracefully in the dance, bends over the horrid burden without a shudder. She gloats over the blood; and just as the maid of your household goes, bearing out on a tray the empty glasses of the evening's entertainment, so she carried out on a platter the disseveled head of that good man, while all the banqueters shouted, and thought it a grand joke, that, in such a brief and easy way, they had freed themselves from such a plain-spoken, troublesome minister.

What could be more innocent than a birthday festival? All the kings from the time of Pharaoh had celebrated such days; and why not Herod? It was right that the palace should be lighted, and that the cymbals should clap, and that the royal guests should go to a banquet; but, before the rioting and wassail that closed the scene of that day, every pure nature revolts.

Behold the work, the influence, and the end of an infamous dancer!

I am, by natural temperament and religious theory, utterly opposed to the position of those who are horrified at every demonstration of mirth and playfulness in social life, and who seem to think that everything, decent and immortal, depends upon the style in which people carry their feet. On the other hand, I can see nothing but ruin, moral and physical, in the dissipations of the ball-room, which have despoiled thousands of young men and women of all that gives dignity to character, or usefulness to life.

Dancing has been styled "the graceful movement of the body adjusted by art, to the measures or tune of instruments, or of the voice. " All nations have danced. The ancients thought that Pollux and Castor at first taught the practice to the Lacedæmonians; but, whatever be its origin, all climes have adopted it.

In other days there were festal dances, and funeral dances, and military dances, and "mediatorial" dances, and bacchanalian dances. Queens and lords have swayed to and fro in their gardens; and the rough men of the backwoods in this way have roused up the echo of the forest. There seems to be something in lively and coherent sounds to evoke the movement of hand and foot, whether cultured or uncultured. Men passing the street unconsciously keep step to the music of the band; and Christians in church unconsciously find themselves keeping time with their feet, while their soul is uplifted by some great harmony. Not only is this true in cultured life, but the red men of Oregon have their scalp dances, and green-corn dances, and war dances. It is, therefore, no abstract question that you ask me—Is it right to dance?

The ancient fathers, aroused by the indecent dances of those days, gave emphatic evidence against any participation in the dance. St. Chrysostom says: —"The feet were not given for dancing, but to walk modestly; not to leap impudently like camels. "

One of the dogmas of the ancient church reads: "A dance is the devil's possession; and he that entereth into a dance, entereth into his possession. The devil is the gate to the middle and to the end of the dance. As many passes as a man makes in dancing, so many passes doth he make to hell. " Elsewhere, these old dogmas declare—"The woman that singeth in the dance is the princess of the devil; and those that answer are his clerks; and the beholders are his friends, and the music are his bellows, and the fiddlers are the ministers of the devil; for, as when hogs are strayed, if the hogs'-herd call one, all assemble together, so the devil calleth one woman to sing in the dance, or to play on some instrument, and presently all the dancers gather together. "

This wholesale and indiscriminate denunciation grew out of the utter dissoluteness of those ancient plays. So great at one time was the offence to all decency, that the Roman Senate decreed the expulsion of all dancers and dancing-masters from Rome.

Yet we are not to discuss the customs of that day, but the customs of the present. We cannot let the fathers decide the question for us. Our reason, enlightened by the Bible, shall be the standard. I am not ready to excommunicate all those who lift their feet beyond a certain height. I would not visit our youth with a rigor of criticism that would put out all their ardor of soul. I do not believe that all the inhabitants of Wales, who used to step to the sound of the rustic pibcorn, went down to ruin. I would give to all of our youth the right to romp and play. God meant it, or he would not have surcharged our natures with such exuberance. If a mother join hands with her children, and while the eldest strikes the keys, fill all the house with the sound of agile feet, I see no harm. If a few friends, gathered in happy circle, conclude to cross and recross the room to the sound of the piano well played, I see no harm. I for a long while tried to see in it a harm, but I never could, and I probably never will. I would to God men kept young for a greater length of time. Never since my school-boy days have I loved so well as now the hilarities of life. What if we have felt heavy burdens, and suffered a multitude of hard knocks, is it any reason why we should stand in the path of those who, unstung by life's misfortunes, are exhilarated and full of glee?

God bless the young! They will have to live many a day if they want to hear me say one word to dampen their ardor or clip their wings, or to throw a cloud upon their life by telling them that it is hard, and dark, and doleful. It is no such thing. You will meet with many a trial; but, speaking from my own experience, let me tell you that you will be treated a great deal better than you deserve.

Let us not grudge to the young their joy. As we go further on in life, let us go with the remembrance that we have had our gleeful days. When old age frosts our locks, and stiffens our limbs, let us not block up the way, but say, "We had our good times: now let others have theirs. " As our children come on, let us cheerfully give them our places. How glad will I be to let them have everything, —my house, my books, my place in society, my heritage! By the time we get old we will have had our way long enough. Then let our children come on and we'll have it their way. For thirty, forty, or fifty years, we have been drinking from the cup of life; and we ought not to complain if called to pass the cup along and let others take a drink.

But, while we have a right to the enjoyments of life, we never will countenance sinful indulgences. I here set forth a group of what might be called the dissipations of the ball-room. They swing an awful scythe of death. Are we to stand idly by, and let the work go on, lest in the rebuke we tread upon the long trail of some popular vanity? The whirlpool of the ball-room drags down the life, the beauty, and the moral worth of the city. In this whirlwind of imported silks goes out the life of many of our best families. Bodies and souls innumerable are annually consumed in this conflagration of ribbons.

This style of dissipation is the abettor of pride, the instigator of jealousy, the sacrificial altar of health, the defiler of the soul, the avenue of lust, and the curse of the town. The tread of this wild, intoxicating, heated midnight dance jars all the moral hearthstones of the city. The physical ruin is evident. What will become of those who work all day and dance all night? A few years will turn them out nervous, exhausted imbeciles. Those who have given up their midnights to spiced wines, and hot suppers, and ride home through winter's cold, unwrapped from the elements, will at last be recorded suicides.

There is but a short step from the ball-room to the grave-yard. There are consumptions and fierce neuralgias close on the track. Amid that glittering maze of ball-room splendors, diseases stand right and left, and balance and chain. A sepulchral breath floats up amid the perfume, and the froth of death's lip bubbles up in the champagne.

Many of our brightest homes are being sacrificed. There are families that have actually quit keeping house, and gone to boarding, that they may give themselves more exclusively to the higher duties of the ball-room. Mothers and daughters, fathers and sons, finding their highest enjoyment in the dance, bid farewell to books, to quiet culture, to all the amenities of home. The father will, after a while, go down into lower dissipations. The son will be tossed about in society, a nonentity. The daughter will elope with a French dancing-master. The mother, still trying to stay in the glitter, and by every art attempting to keep the color in her cheek, and the wrinkles off her brow, attempting, without any success, all the arts of the belle, —an old flirt, a poor, miserable butterfly without any wings.

If anything on the earth is beautiful to my eye, it is an aged woman; her hair floating back over the wrinkled brow, not frosted, but white with the blossoms of the tree of life; her voice tender with past memories, and her face a benediction. The children pull at grandmother's dress as she passes through the room, and almost pull her down in her weakness; yet she has nothing but a cake, or a candy, or a kind word for the little darlings. When she goes away from us there is a shadow on the table, a shadow on the hearth, and a shadow in the dwelling.

But if anything on earth is distressful to look at, it is an old woman ashamed of being old. What with paint and false hair, she is too much for my gravity. I laugh, even in church, when I see her coming. One of the worst looking birds I know of is a peacock after it has lost its feathers. I would not give one lock of my mother's gray hair for fifty thousand such caricatures of old age. The first time you find these faithful disciples of the ball-room diligently engaged and happy in the duties of the home circle, send me word, for I would go a great way to see such a phenomenon. These creatures have no home. Their children unwashed. Their furniture undusted. Their china closets disordered. The house a scene of confusion, misrule, cheerlessness, and dirt. One would think you might discover even amid the witcheries of the ball-room the sickening odors of the unswept, unventilated, and unclean domestic apartments.

These dissipations extinguish all love of usefulness. How could you expect one to be interested in the alleviations of the world's misery, while there is a question to be decided about the size of a glove or the shade of a pongee? How many of these men and women of the ball-room visit the poor, or help dress the wounds of a returned soldier in the hospital? When did the world ever see a perpetual dancer distributing tracts? Such persons are turned in upon themselves. And it is very poor pasture!

This gilded sphere is utterly bedwarfing to intellect and soul. This constant study of little things; this harassing anxiety about dress; this talk of fashionable infinitesimals; this shoe-pinched, hair-frizzled, fringe-spattered group—that simper and look askance at the mirrors and wonder, with infinity of interest, "how that one geranium leaf does look; " this shrivelling up of man's moral dignity, until it is no more observable with the naked eye; this taking of a woman's heart, that God meant should be filled with all amenities, and compressing it until all the fragrance, and simplicity, and artlessness are squeezed out of it; this inquisition of a small shoe; this agony of tight lacing; this wrapping up of mind and heart in a ruffle; this tumbling down of a soul that God meant for great upliftings!

I prophesy the spiritual ruin of all participators in this rivalry. Have the white, polished, glistening boards ever been the road to heaven? Who at the flash of those chandeliers hath kindled a torch for eternity? From the table spread at the close of that excited and besweated scene, who went home to say his prayers?

To many, alas! this life is a masquerade ball. As, at such entertainments, gentlemen and ladies appear in the dress of kings or queens, mountain bandits or clowns, and at the close of the dance throw off their disguises, so, in this dissipated life, all unclean passions move in mask. Across the floor they trip merrily. The lights sparkle along the wall, or drop from the ceiling—a very cohort of fire! The music charms. The diamonds glitter. The feet bound. Gemmed hands, stretched out, clasp gemmed hands. Dancing feet respond to dancing feet. Gleaming brow bends low to gleaming brow. On with the dance! Flash, and rustle, and laughter, and immeasurable merry-making! But the languor of death comes over the limbs, and blurs the sight. *Lights lower!* Floor hollow with sepulchral echo. Music saddens into a wail. *Lights lower!* The maskers can hardly now be seen. Flowers exchange their fragrance for a sickening odor, such as comes from garlands that have lain in vaults of cemeteries. *Lights lower!* Mists fill the room. Glasses rattle as though shaken by sullen thunder. Sighs seem caught among the curtains. Scarf falls from the shoulder of beauty, —a shroud! *Lights lower!* Over the slippery boards, in dance of death, glide jealousies, disappointments, lust, despair. Torn leaves and withered garlands only half hide the ulcered feet. The stench of smoking lamp-wicks almost quenched. Choking damps. Chilliness. Feet still. Hands folded. Eyes shut. Voices hushed.

LIGHTS OUT!

THE MASSACRE BY NEEDLE AND SEWING-MACHINE.

Very long ago the needle was busy. It was considered honorable for women to toil in olden time. Alexander the Great stood in his palace showing garments made by his own mother. The finest tapestries at Bayeux were made by the Queen of William the Conqueror. Augustus the Emperor would not wear any garments except those that were fashioned by some member of his royal family. So let the toiler everywhere be respected!

The greatest blessing that could have happened to our first parents was being turned out of Eden after they had done wrong. Adam and Eve, in their perfect state, might have got along without work, or only such slight employment as a perfect garden, with no weeds in it, demanded. But, as soon as they had sinned, the best thing for them was to be turned out where they would have to work. We know what a withering thing it is for a man to have nothing to do. Old Ashbel Green, at fourscore years, when asked why he kept on working, said, "I do so to keep out of mischief. " We see that a man who has a large amount of money to start with has no chance. Of the thousand prosperous and honorable men that you know, nine hundred and ninety-nine had to work vigorously at the beginning.

But I am now to tell you that industry is just as important for a woman's safety and happiness. The most unhappy women in our communities to-day are those who have no engagements to call them up in the morning; who, once having risen and breakfasted, lounge through the dull forenoon in slippers down at the heel and with dishevelled hair, reading George Sand's last novel; and who, having dragged through a wretched forenoon and taken their afternoon sleep, and having spent an hour and a half at their toilet, pick up their card-case and go out to make calls; and who pass their evenings waiting for somebody to come in and break up the monotony. Arabella Stuart never was imprisoned in so dark a dungeon as that.

There is no happiness in an idle woman. It may be with hand, it may be with brain, it may be with foot; but work she must, or be wretched forever. The little girls of our families must be started with that idea. The curse of our American society is that our young women are taught that the first, second, third, fourth, fifth, sixth, seventh, tenth, fiftieth, thousandth thing in their life is to get somebody to take care of them. Instead of that, the first lesson should be, how, under God, they may take care of themselves. The simple fact is that a majority of them do have to take care of themselves, and that, too, after having, through the false notions of their parents, wasted the years in which they ought to have learned how successfully to maintain themselves. We now and here declare the inhumanity, cruelty, and outrage of that father and mother, who pass their daughters into womanhood, having given them no facility for earning their livelihood. Madame de Staël said: "It is not these writings that I am proud of, but the fact that I have facility in ten occupations, in any one of which I could make a livelihood. "

You say you have a fortune to leave them. O man and woman! have you not learned that, like vultures, like hawks, like eagles, riches have wings and fly away? Though you should be successful in leaving a competency behind you, the trickery of executors may swamp it in a night; or some elders or deacons of our churches may get up an oil company, or some sort of religious enterprise sanctioned by the church, and induce your orphans to put their money into a hole in Venango County; and if, by the most skilful derricks, the sunken money cannot be pumped up again, prove to them that it was eternally decreed that that was the way they were to lose it, and that it went in the most orthodox and heavenly style.

O the damnable schemes that professed Christians will engage in—until God puts his fingers into the collar of the hypocrite's robe and rips it clear down to the bottom!

You have no right, because you are well off, to conclude that your children are going to be as well off. A man died, leaving a large fortune. His son, a few months ago, fell dead in a Philadelphia grog-shop. His old comrades came in and said, as they bent over his corpse: "What is the matter with you, Boggsey? " The surgeon standing over him said: "Hush up! he is dead! " —"Ah, he is dead! " they said. "Come, boys, let us go and take a drink in memory of poor Boggsey! "

Have you nothing better than money to leave your children? If you have not, but send your daughters into the world with empty brain and unskilled hand, you are guilty of assassination, homicide, regicide, infanticide—compared with which that of poor Hester Vaughan was innocence. There are women toiling in our cities for three and four dollars per week, who were the daughters of merchant princes. These suffering ones now would be glad to have the crumbs that once fell from their father's table. That worn-out, broken shoe that she wears is the lineal descendant of the twelve-dollar gaiters in which her mother walked; and that torn and faded calico had ancestry of magnificent brocade, that swept Broadway clean without any expense to the street commissioners. Though you live in an elegant residence, and fare sumptuously every day, let your daughters feel it is a disgrace to them not to know how to work. I denounce the idea, prevalent in society, that though our young women may embroider slippers, and crochet, and make mats for lamps to stand on, without disgrace, the idea of doing anything for a livelihood is dishonorable. It is a shame for a young woman, belonging to a large family, to be inefficient when the father toils his life away for her support. It is a shame for a daughter to be idle while her mother toils at the wash-tub. It is as honorable to sweep house, make beds, or trim hats, as it is to twist a watch-chain.

As far as I can understand, the line of respectability lies between that which is useful and that which is useless. If women do that which is of no value, their work is honorable. If they do practical work, it is dishonorable. That our young women may escape the censure of doing dishonorable work, I shall particularize. You may knit a tidy for the back of an armchair, but by no means make the money wherewith to buy the chair. You may, with delicate brush, beautify a mantel-ornament, but die rather than earn enough to buy a marble mantel. You may learn artistic music until you can squall Italian, but never sing "Ortonville" or "Old Hundred. " Do nothing practical, if you would, in the eyes of refined society, preserve your respectability.

I scout these finical notions. I tell you a woman, no more than a man, has a right to occupy a place in this world unless she pays a rent for it.

In the course of a lifetime you consume whole harvests, and droves of cattle, and every day you live breathe forty hogsheads of good pure air. You must, by some kind of usefulness, *pay* for all this. Our race was the last thing created, —the birds and fishes on the fourth day, the cattle and lizards on the fifth day, and man on the sixth day. If geologists are right, the earth was a million of years in the possession of the insects, beasts, and birds, before our race came upon it. In one sense, we were innovators. The cattle, the lizards, and the hawks had pre-emption right. The question is not what we are to do with the lizards and summer insects, but what the lizards and summer insects are to do with us.

If we want a place in this world we must *earn* it. The partridge makes its own nest before it occupies it. The lark, by its morning song, earns its breakfast before it eats it; and the Bible gives an intimation that the first duty of an idler is to starve, when it says if he "will not work, neither shall he eat. " Idleness ruins the health; and very soon Nature says, "This man has refused to pay his rent; out with him! "

Society is to be reconstructed on the subject of woman's toil. A vast majority of those who would have woman industrious shut her up to a few kinds of work. My judgment in this matter is, that a woman has a right to do anything she can do well. There should be no department of merchandise, mechanism, art, or science barred against her. If Miss Hosmer has genius for sculpture, give her a chisel. If Rosa Bonheur has a fondness for delineating animals, let her make "The Horse Fair. " If Miss Mitchell will study astronomy, let her mount the starry ladder. If Lydia will be a merchant, let her sell purple. If Lucretia Mott will preach the Gospel, let her thrill with her womanly eloquence the Quaker meeting-house.

It is said, if woman is given such opportunities, she will occupy places that might be taken by men. I say, if she have more skill and adaptedness for any position than a man has, let her have it! She has as much right to her bread, to her apparel, and to her home, as men have.

But it is said that her nature is so delicate that she is unfitted for exhausting toil. I ask, in the name of all past history, what toil on earth is more severe, exhausting, and tremendous than that toil of the needle to which for ages she has been subjected? The battering-ram, the sword, the carbine, the battle-axe have made no such havoc as the needle. I would that these living sepulchres in which women have for ages been buried might be opened, and that some resurrection trumpet might bring up these living corpses to the fresh air and sunlight.

Go with me, and I will show you a woman who, by hardest toil, supports her children, her drunken husband, her old father and mother, pays her house-rent, always has wholesome food on her table, and, when she can get some neighbor on the Sabbath to come in and take care of her family, appears in church, with hat and cloak that are far from indicating the toil to which she is subjected.

Such a woman as that has body and soul enough to fit her for *any* position. She could stand beside the majority of your salesmen and dispose of more goods. She could go into your wheelwright shops and beat one-half of your workmen at making carriages. We talk about woman as though we had resigned to her all the light work, and ourselves had shouldered the heavier. But the day of judgment, which will reveal the sufferings of the stake and inquisition, will marshal before the throne of God and the hierarchs of heaven the martyrs of wash-tub and needle.

Now, I say, if there be any preference in occupation, let woman have it. God knows her trials are the severest. By her acuter sensitiveness to misfortune, by her hour of anguish, I demand that no one hedge up her pathway to a livelihood. O the meanness, the despicability of men who begrudge a woman the right to work anywhere, in any honorable calling!

I go still further, and say that women should have equal compensation with men. By what principle of justice is it that women in many of our cities get only two-thirds as much pay as men, and in many cases only half? Here is the gigantic injustice— that for work equally well, if not better done, woman receives far less compensation than man. Start with the National Government: women clerks in Washington get nine hundred dollars for doing that for which men receive eighteen hundred.

To thousands of young women of New York to-day there is only this alternative: starvation or dishonor. Many of the largest mercantile establishments of our cities are accessory to these abominations; and from their large establishments there are scores of souls being pitched off into death; *and their employers know it!*

Is there a God? Will there be a judgment? I tell you, if God rises up to redress woman's wrongs, many of our large establishments will be swallowed up quicker than a South-American earthquake ever took down a city. God will catch these oppressors between the two mill-stones of his wrath, and grind them to powder!

The Abominations of Modern Society

Why is it that a female principal in a school gets only eight hundred and twenty-five dollars for doing work for which a male principal gets sixteen hundred and fifty?

I hear from all this land the wail of woman-hood. Man has nothing to answer to that wail but flatteries. He says she is an angel. She is not. She knows she is not. She is a human being, who gets hungry when she has no food, and cold when she has no fire. Give her no more flatteries: give her *justice!*

There are thirty-five thousand sewing-girls in New York and Brooklyn. Across the darkness of this night I hear their death-groan. It is not such a cry as comes from those who are suddenly hurled out of life, but a slow, grinding, horrible wasting away. Gather them before you and look into their faces, pinched, ghastly, hunger-struck! Look at their fingers, needle-picked and blood-tipped! See that premature stoop in the shoulders! Hear that dry, hacking, merciless cough!

At a large meeting of these women, held in a hall in Philadelphia, grand speeches were delivered, but a needle-woman took the stand, threw aside her faded shawl, and, with her shrivelled arm, hurled a very thunder-bolt of eloquence, speaking out of the horrors of her own experience.

Stand at the corner of a street in New York at half-past five or six o'clock in the morning, as the women go to their work. Many of them had no breakfast except the crumbs that were left over from the night before, or a crust they chew on their way through the street. Here they come! the working girls of New York and Brooklyn! These engaged in bead-work, these in flower-making, in millinery, enamelling, cigar making, book-binding, labelling, feather-picking, print-coloring, paper-box making, but, most overworked of all, and least compensated, the sewing-women. Why do they not take the city-cars on their way up? They cannot afford the five cents! If, concluding to deny herself something else, she get into the car, give her a seat! You want to see how Latimer and Ridley appeared in the fire: look at that woman and behold a more horrible martyrdom, a hotter fire, a more agonizing death! Ask that woman how much she gets for her work, and she will tell you six cents for making coarse shirts, and finds her own thread!

Last Sabbath night, in the vestibule of my church, after service, a woman fell in convulsions. The doctor said she needed medicine not so much as something to eat. As she began to revive in her delirium, she said, gaspingly: "Eight cents! Eight cents! Eight cents! I wish I could get it done! I am so tired! I wish I could get some sleep, but I must get it done! Eight cents! Eight cents! " We found afterwards that she was making garments for eight cents apiece, and that she could make but three of them in a day! Hear it! Three times eight are twenty-four! Hear it, men and women who have comfortable homes!

Some of the worst villains of the city are the employers of these women. They beat them down to the last penny, and try to cheat them out of that. The woman must deposit a dollar or two before she gets the garments to work on. When the work is done it is sharply inspected, the most insignificant flaws picked out, and the wages refused, and sometimes the dollar deposited not given back. The Women's Protective Union reports a case where one of these poor souls, finding a place where she could get more wages, resolved to change employers, and went to get her pay for work done. The employer says: "I hear you are going to leave me? " — "Yes, " she said, "and I have come to get what you owe me. " He made no answer. She said: "Are you not going to pay me? " — "Yes, " he said, "I will pay you; " and *he kicked her down the stairs.*

How are these evils to be eradicated? What have you to answer, you who sell coats, and have shoes made, and contract for the Southern and Western markets? What help is there, what panacea, what redemption? Some say: "Give women the ballot. " What effect such ballot might have on other questions I am not here to discuss; but what would be the effect of female suffrage upon woman's wages? I do not believe that woman will ever get justice by woman's ballot.

Indeed, women oppress women as much as men do. Do not women, as much as men, beat down to the lowest figure the woman who sews for them? Are not women as sharp as men on washerwomen, and milliners, and mantua-makers? If a woman asks a dollar for her work, does not her female employer ask her if she will not take ninety cents? You say "only ten cents difference; " but that is sometimes the difference between heaven and hell. Women often have less commiseration for women than men. If a woman steps aside from the path of virtue, man may forgive, — woman never! Woman will never get justice done her from woman's ballot.

Neither will she get it from man's ballot. How, then? God will rise up for her. God has more resources than we know of. The flaming sword that hung at Eden's gate when woman was driven out will cleave with its terrible edge her oppressors.

But there is something for our women to do. Let our young people prepare to excel in spheres of work, and they will be able, after a while, to get larger wages. If it be shown that a woman can, in a store, sell more goods in a year than a man, she will soon be able not only to ask but to *demand* more wages, and to demand them successfully. Unskilled and incompetent labor must take what is given; skilled and competent labor will eventually make its own standard. Admitting that the law of supply and demand regulates these things, I contend that the demand for skilled labor is very great, and the supply very small.

Start with the idea that work is *honorable*, and that you can do some one thing better than any one else. Resolve that, God helping, you will take care of yourself. If you are, after a while, called into another relation, you will all the better be qualified for it by your spirit of self-reliance; or if you are called to stay as you are, you can be happy and self-supporting.

Poets are fond of talking about man as an oak, and woman the vine that climbs it; but I have seen many a tree fall that not only went down itself, but took all the vines with it. I can tell you of something stronger than an oak for an ivy to climb on, and that is the throne of the great Jehovah. Single or affianced, that woman is strong who leans on God and does her best. The needle may break; the factory-band may slip; the wages may fail; but, over every good woman's head there are spread the two great, gentle, stupendous wings of the Almighty.

Many of you will go single-handed through life, and you will have to choose between two characters. Young woman, I am sure you will turn your back upon the useless, giggling, painted nonentity which society ignominiously acknowledges to be a woman, and ask God to make you an humble, active, earnest Christian.

What will become of this godless disciple of fashion? What an insult to her sex! Her manners are an outrage upon decency. She is more thoughtful of the attitude she strikes upon the carpet than how she will look in the judgment; more worried about her freckles than her sins; more interested in her bonnet-strings than in her redemption. Her apparel is the poorest part of a Christian woman, however magnificently dressed, and no one has so much right to dress well as a Christian. Not so with the godless disciple of fashion. Take her robes, and you take everything. Death will come down on her some day, and rub the bistre off her eyelids, and the rouge off her cheeks, and with two rough, bony hands, scatter spangles and glass beads and rings and ribbons and lace and brooches and buckles and sashes and frisettes and golden clasps.

The dying actress whose life had been vicious said: "The scene closes. Draw the curtain. " Generally the tragedy comes first, and the farce afterward; but in her life it was first the farce of a useless life, and then the tragedy of a wretched eternity.

Compare the life and death of such an one with that of some Christian aunt that was once a blessing to your household. I do not know that she was ever offered the hand in marriage. She lived single, that untrammelled she might be everybody's blessing. Whenever the sick were to be visited, or the poor to be provided with bread, she went with a blessing. She could pray, or sing "Rock of Ages, " for any sick pauper who asked her. As she got older, there were days when she was a little sharp, but for the most part Auntie was a sunbeam—just the one for Christmas-eve. She knew better than any one else how to fix things. Her every prayer, as God heard it, was full of everybody who had trouble. The brightest things in all the house dropped from her fingers. She had peculiar notions, but the grandest notion she ever had was to make you happy. She dressed well—Auntie always dressed well; but her highest adornment was that of a meek and quiet spirit, which, in the sight of God, is of great price. When she died, you all gathered lovingly about her; and as you carried her out to rest, the Sunday-school class almost covered the coffin with japonicas; and the poor people stood at the end of the alley, with their aprons to their eyes, sobbing bitterly; and the man of the world said, with Solomon, "Her price was above rubies; " and Jesus, as unto the maiden in Judea, commanded: "I SAY UNTO THEE, ARISE! "

PICTURES IN THE STOCK GALLERY.

[NOTE. —This chapter, though largely devoted to "Oil, " is to be construed as reaching any other "Kite" that the stock gambler flies— any other scheme which his unprincipled ideas of right and wrong will permit him to work to his own gain and others' loss. The oil mania was only a more popular or attractive *vice* of the stock-boards, which is reproduced, in spirit and motive, almost every month of the year.]

At my entrance upon this discussion, I must deplore the indiscriminate terms of condemnation employed by many well-meaning persons in regard to stock operations. The business of the stock-broker is just as legitimate and necessary as that of a dealer in clothes, groceries, or hardware; and a man may be as pure-minded and holy a Christian at the Board of Brokers as in a prayer-meeting. The broker is, in the sight of God, as much entitled to his commissions as any hard-working mechanic is entitled to his day's wages. Any man has as much right to make money by the going up of stocks as by the going up of sugar, rice, or tea. The inevitable board-book that the operator carries in his hand may be as pure as the clothing merchant's ledger. It is the work of the brokers to facilitate business; to make transfer of investment; to watch and report the tides of business; to assist the merchant in lawful enterprises.

Because there are men in this department of business, sharp, deceitful, and totally iniquitous, you have no right to denounce the entire class. Importers, shoe-dealers, lumbermen, do not want to be held responsible for the moral deficits of their comrades in business. Neither have you a right to excoriate those who are conscientiously operating through the channels spoken of. If they take a risk, so do all business men. The merchant who buys silk at five dollars per yard takes his chances; he expects it to go up to six dollars; it may fall to four dollars. If a man, by straightforward operations in stocks, meets with disaster and fails, he deserves sympathy just as much as he who sold spices or calicoes, and through some miscalculation is struck down bankrupt.

We have no right to impose restrictions upon this class of men that we impose upon no other. What right have you to denounce the operation "buyer—ten days" or "buyer—twenty days, " when you take a house, "buyer—three hundred and sixty-five days? " Perhaps the entire payment is to be made at the end of a year, when you do not know but that, by that time, you will be penniless. Give all men their due, if you would hold beneficent influence over them. Do not be too rough in pulling out the weeds, lest you uproot also the marigolds and verbenas. In the Board of Brokers there are some of the most conscientious, upright Christian men of our cities—men who would scorn a lie, or a subterfuge. Indeed, there are men in these boards who might, in some respects, teach a lesson of morality to other commercial circles.

I will not deny that there are special temptations connected with this business even when carried on legitimately. So there are dangers to the engineer on a railroad. He does not know what night he may dash into the coal-train. But engines must be run, and stocks must be sold. A nervous, excitable man ought to be very slow to undertake either the engine or the Stock Exchange.

A clever young man, of twenty-five years of age, bought ten shares in the Pennsylvania Central Railroad. The stock went up five dollars per share, and he made fifty dollars by the operation. His mother, knowing his temperament, said to him, "I wish you had lost it. " But, encouraged, he entered another operation, and took ten shares in another railroad and made two hundred dollars. By this time he was ready for the wildest scheme. He lost, in three years, forty thousand dollars, ruined his health, and broke his wife's heart. Her father supports them chiefly now. The unfortunate has a shingle up, in a small court, among low operators. Such a man as this is unfit for this commercial sphere. He would have been unfit for a pilot, unfit for military command, unfit for any place that demands steady nerve, cool brain, and well-balanced temperament.

But, while there is a legitimate sphere for the broker and operator, there are transactions every day undertaken in our cities that can only be characterized as superb outrage and villany; and there are members of Christian churches who have been guilty of speculations that, in the last day, will blanch their cheek, and thunder them down to everlasting companionship with the lowest gamblers that ever pitched pennies for a drink.

It is not necessary that I should draw the difficult line between honorable and dishonorable speculation. God has drawn it through every man's conscience. The broker guilty of "cornering" as well knows that he is sinning against God and man, as though the flame of Mount Sinai singed his eyebrows. He hears that a brother broker has sold "short, " and immediately goes about with a wise look, saying: "Erie is going down—Erie is going down; prepare for it. " Immediately the people begin to sell; he buys up the stock; monopolizes the whole affair; drags down the man who sold short; makes largely, pockets the gain, and thanks the Lord for great prosperity in business. You call it "cornering." I call it gambling, theft, highway robbery, villany accursed.

It is astonishing how some men, who are kind in their families, useful in the church, charitable to the poor, are utterly transformed of the devil as soon as they enter the Stock Exchange. A respectable member of one of the churches of the city went into a broker's office and said: "Get me one hundred shares of Reading, and carry it; I will leave a margin of five hundred dollars. " Instead of going up, according to anticipation, the stock fell. Every few days the operator called to ask the broker what success. The stock still declined. The operator was so terribly excited that the broker asked him what was the matter. He replied: "To tell you the truth, I borrowed that five hundred dollars that I lost, and, in anticipation of what I was sure I was going to get by the operation, I made a very large subscription to the Missionary Society."

The nation has become so accustomed to frauds that no astonishment is excited thereby. The public conscience has for many years been utterly debauched by what were called fancy stocks, morus multicaulis, Western city enterprises, and New England developments.

If a man find on his farm something as large as the head of a pin, that, in a strong sunlight, sparkles a little, a gold company is formed; books are opened; working capital declared; a select number go in on the "ground floor; " and the estates of widows and orphans are swept into the vortex. Very little discredit is connected with any such transaction, if it is only on a large scale. We cannot bear small and insignificant dishonesties, but take off our hats and bow almost to the ground in the presence of the man who has made one hundred thousand dollars by one swindle. A woman was arrested in the streets of one of our cities for selling molasses candy on Sunday. She was tried, condemned, and imprisoned. Coming out of prison, she went into the same business and sold molasses candy on Sunday. Again she was arrested, condemned, and imprisoned. On coming out—showing the total depravity of a woman's heart—she again went into the same business, and sold molasses candy on Sunday. Whereupon the police, the mayor and the public sentiment of the city rose up and declared that, though the heavens fell, no woman should be allowed to sell molasses candy on Sunday. Yet the law puts its hands behind its back, and walks up and down in the presence of a thousand abominations and dares not whisper.

There are scores of men to-day on the streets, whose costly family wardrobes, whose rosewood furniture, whose splendid turn-outs, whose stately mansions, are made out of the distresses of sewing-women, whose money they gathered up in a stock swindle. There is human sweat in the golden tankards. There is human blood in the crimson plush. There are the bones of unrequited toil in the pearly keys of the piano. There is the curse of an incensed God hovering over all their magnificence. Some night the man will not be able to rest. He will rise up in bewilderment and look about him, crying: "Who is there? " Those whom he has wronged will thrust their skinny arms under the tapestry, and touch his brow, and feel for his heart, and blow their sepulchral breath into his face, crying: "Come to judgment!"

For the warning of young men, I shall specify but two of the world's most gigantic swindles—one English, and the other American. In England, in the early part of the last century, reports were circulated of the fabulous wealth of South America. A company was formed, with a stock of what would be equal to thirty millions of our dollars. The government guaranteed to the company the control of all the trade to the South Sea, and the company was to assume the entire debt of England, then amounting to one hundred and forty millions of dollars. Magnificent project! The English nation talked and dreamed of nothing but Peruvian gold and Mexican silver, the national debt liquidated, and Eldorados numberless and illimitable! When five million pounds of new stock was offered at three hundred pounds per share, it was all snatched up with avidity. Thirty million dollars of the stock was subscribed for, when there were but five millions offered. South Sea went up, until in the midsummer month the stock stood at one thousand per cent. The whole nation was intoxicated. Around about this scheme, as might have been expected, others just as wild arose. A company was formed with ten million dollars of capital for importing walnut trees from Virginia. A company for developing a wheel to go by perpetual motion, with a capital of four million dollars. A company for developing a new kind of soap. A company for insuring against losses by servants, with fifteen million dollars capital. One scheme was entitled: "A company for carrying on an undertaking of great advantage, but nobody to know what it is—capital two million five hundred thousand dollars, in shares of five hundred each. Further information to be given in a month. "

The books were opened at nine o'clock in the morning. Before night a thousand shares were taken, and two thousand pounds paid in. So successful was the day's work, that that night the projector of the enterprise went out of the business, and forever vanished from the public. But it was not a perfect loss. The subscribers had their ornamented certificates of stock to comfort them. Hunt's Merchant's Magazine, speaking of those times, says "that from morning until evening 'Change Alley was filled to overflowing with one dense mass of living beings composed of the most incongruous materials, and, in all things save the mad pursuit in which they were employed, the very opposite in habits and conditions. "

What was the end of this chapter of English enterprise? Suddenly the ruin came. Down went the whole nation—members of Parliament, tradesmen, physicians, clergymen, lawyers, royal ladies, and poor needle-women—in one stupendous calamity. The whole earth, and all the ages, heard that bubble burst.

But I am not through. Our young men shall hear more startling things. We surpass England in having higher mountains, deeper rivers, greater cataracts, and larger armies. Yea, we have surpassed it in magnitude of swindles. I wish to unfold before the young men of the country, and before those in whose hands may now be the price of blood, the wide-spread, ghastly, and almost infinitely greater wickedness of the gamblers in oil stock. Now, the obtaining of lands, the transporting of machinery, and the forming of companies for the production of oil, is just as honorable as any organization for the obtaining of coal, iron, copper, or zinc. God poured out before this nation a river of oil, and intended us to gather it up, transport it, and use it; and there were companies formed that have withstood all commercial changes, and continued, year after year, in the prosecution of an honorable business. I have just as much respect for the man who has made fifty thousand dollars by oil as I have for him who has made it by spices.

Out of twelve hundred petroleum companies, how many do you suppose were honestly formed and rightfully conducted? Do you say six hundred? You make large demands upon one's credulity; but let us be generous, and suppose that six hundred companies bought land, issued honest circulars, sent out machinery, and plunged into the earth for the rightful development of resources. To form the other six hundred companies, only three or four things were necessary: First, an attractive circular, regardless of expense. It must have all the colors and hues of earth, and sea, and heaven. Let the letters flame with all the beauty of gold, and jasper, and amethyst. It must state the date of incorporation, and the fact that "all subscribers shall get the benefit of the original undertaking. While it does not make so much pretension as some other companies, it must be distinctly announced that this is a safe and permanent investment. " The circular must state that "there are a goodly number of flowing wells, and others which the company are happy to say have a very good smell of oil. " "The books will be open only five days, as there are only a few shares yet to be taken. " Connected with this circular is an elaborate map, drawn by the artist of the company. Never mind the geography of the country. Our map must have a creek running through it, so crooked as to traverse as much of the land as possible, and make it all water-front. "Ah! " said one man to his artist, "you make only one creek. "—"Well, " said the artist, "if you want three creeks you can have them at very little expense. There—you have them now—three creeks! "

Then the circular must have good names attached to it. How to get them? The president and directors must be prominent men. If celebrated for piety, all the better. The estimable man approached says: "I know nothing about this company. "—"Well, " says the committee waiting on him, "we will give you five hundred dollars' worth of shares. " Immediately the estimable man begins to "know about it," and accepts the position of president. Three or four directors are obtained in the same way. Now the thing is easy. After this you can get anybody. Ordinary Christians and sinners feel it a joy to be in such celebrated society.

Another thing important is that the company purchase three or four vials of oil to stand in the window—some in the crude state, the rest clarified. Genuine specimens from Venango County.

Another important thing: there must be a large working capital, for the company do not mean to be idle. They have derricks already building; and there will be large monthly dividends. Let it be known that there were companies in some cities who, claiming to have a capital of four hundred thousand dollars, yet had that capital exhausted when they had sunk one well costing five thousand dollars. But never mind. The thing must be right, for some of the directors are eminent for respectability. You say it is certainly important that there be some land out of which the oil is to be obtained. Oh! no. Why be troubled with any land at all? It is an expense for nothing. You have the circular, and the glowing map, with the creeks and three vials of oil in the window, and a flaming advertisement in the newspapers. Now let the books be opened! Better if you can have a half-dozen offices in one room; then the agent can accommodate you with anything you desire. If you want to take a "flyer" in this and a "flyer" in that, you shall have it.

Coming in from the country are farmers, dairymen, day-laborers. Great chances now for speedy emoluments. Pour in the hard-earned treasures. Sure enough, a dividend of one per cent. per month! Forthwith, another multitude are convinced of the safety of the investment. The second month another dividend. The third month another. Whence do these dividends come? From the product of the wells? Oh! no. It is your own money they are paying you back. How generous of this company to give you five dollars back, when you might have lost it all!

But the dividends stop. What is the matter? Instead of the advertisement which covered a whole column of the newspapers, there comes a modest little notice that "a special meeting of the stockholders will be held for the purpose of transacting business of importance. " Perhaps it may be to assess the stockholders for the purpose of keeping the little land they have, if they have any. Or it may be for the election of a new group of officers, for the present incumbents do not want to be always before the public. They are modest men. They believe in rotation of office. They cannot consent any longer to serve. Where have they gone to? They are busy putting up a princely mansion at Long Branch, Germantown, or Chelsea. They have served their day and generation, and have gone to their flocks and herds. Where is the Church of God, that she allows in her membership such gigantic abominations? Were the thirty pieces of silver that Judas received denounced as unfit, and shall the Church of God have nothing to say about this price of blood? Is sin to be excused because it is as high as heaven, or deep as hell? The man who allows his name to be used as president or director in connection with an enterprise that he knows is to result in the sale of twenty thousand shares of an undeveloped nothing—God will tear off the cloak of his hypocrisy, and in the last day show him to all the universe—a brazen-faced gambler. His house will be accursed. God's anathemas will flash in the chandelier, and rattle in the swift hoofs of his silver-bitted grays; and the day of fire will see him willing to leap into a burning oil-well to hide himself from the face of the Lamb. The hundred thousand dollars gotten in unrighteousness will not be enough to build a barricade against the advance of the divine judgments.

Think of the elder in a church who, from the oil regions, sends an exciting telegram, so that one man buys a large amount of stock at twelve, on Wednesday. The next day it is put on the stock-board at six. The enterprising man, who sold it at twelve, goes out to buy one of the grandest estates within ten miles of the city. The man who bought it goes into the dust; and the secret gets out that the exciting telegram sent by the elder arose, not from any oil actually discovered, but because in boring they had found a magnificent odor of oil.

If he who steals a dollar from a money-drawer is a thief, then he who by dishonesty gets five hundred thousand dollars is five hundred thousand times more a thief. And so the last day will declare him.

Did not the law right the injured man? No! The poor who were wronged would not undertake a suit against a company that could bring fifty thousand dollars to the enlightenment of judge, jury, and lawyer; while, on the other hand, the affluent who had been gouged would not go to the courts for justice. Why! how would it sound, if it got out, that Mr. So and So, one of the first merchants on Wall, or Third, or State street, had got swindled? They will keep it still.

The guilty range to-day undisturbed through society, and will continue to do so until the Lord God shall bring them to an unerring settlement, and proclaim to an astonished universe how many lies they told about the land, about the derricks, about the yield, about the dividends. What shall such an one say, when God shall, in the great day of account, hold up before him the circular, and the map, and the newspaper advertisement? Speechless!

Before that day shall come I warn you—Disgorge! you infamous stock gamblers! Gather together so many of your company as have any honesty left, and join in the following circular: —*"We the undersigned, do hereby repent of our villainies, and beg pardon of the public for all the wrongs that we have done them; and hereby ask the widows and orphans whom we have made penniless to come next Saturday, between ten and three o'clock, and receive back what we stole from them. We hereby confess that the wells spoken of in our circular never yielded any oil; and that the creeks running through our ornamented map were an entire fiction; and that the elder who piously rolled up his eyes and said it was a safe investment, was not as devout as he looked to be. Signed by the subscribers at their office, in the year of our Lord 1871."*

Then your conscience will be clear, and you can die in peace. But I have no faith in such a reformation. When the devil gets such a fair hold of a man he hardly ever lets go.

To the young I turn and utter a word of warning. While you are determined to be acute business men, resolve at the very threshold that you will have nothing to do with stock-*gambling*. This country can richly afford to lose the eight hundred millions of dollars swindled out of honest people, if our young men, by it, will be warned for all the future. Think you such enterprises are forever passed away? No! they begin already to clamor for public attention and patronage. There are now hundreds of printing-presses busy in making pamphlets and circulars for schemes as hollow and nefarious as those I have mentioned. There are silver-mining companies, founded upon nobody knows what—to accomplish what, nobody cares. There will be other Canada gold companies; there will be other copper-mining companies; there will be more mutual consumers' coal companies, who, not satisfied with the price of ordinary coal-dealers, will resolve themselves into consumers' associations, where the thing consumed is not the coal, but themselves—the companies that were to be immaculate, setting the whole community to playing the game of "Who's got the money?"

Stand off from all *doubtful* enterprises! Resolve that if, in a lawful way, you cannot earn a living, then you will die an honest man, and be buried in an honest sepulchre.

There are two or three reasons why you should have nothing to do with such operations. Mentioning the lowest motive first, it will desolate you financially. I asked a man of large observation and undoubted integrity, how many of the professed stock-gamblers made a *permanent* fortune. He answered, "Not one! not one of those who made this their only business. " For a little while you may plunge in a round of seeming prosperity; but your money is put into a bag with holes. You cannot successfully bury a dishonest dollar. You may put it down into the very heart of the earth; you may heave rocks upon the top of it; on top of the rocks you may put banks and all moneyed institutions, but that dishonest dollar beneath will begin to heave and toss and upturn itself, and keep on until it comes to the resurrection of damnation.

Then this stock-gambling life is wretchedly unhappy. It makes the nerves shake, and the brain hot, and the heart sad, and the life disquieted.

A man in Philadelphia, who seems to be an exception to the rule—that such men do not permanently prosper—who has well on towards a million of dollars, and is nearly seventy years of age, may be seen, every day, going in and out, eaten up of stocks, torn in an inquisition of stocks, rode by a nightmare of stocks; and, with the earnestness of a drowning man, he rushes into a broker's shop, crying out: "Did you get me those shares? " In such an anxious, exciting life there are griefs, disappointments, anguish, but there is no happiness.

Worse than all, it destroys the soul. The day must come when the worthless scrip will fall out of the clutches of the stock-gambler. Satan will play upon him the "cornering" game which, down on Wall street, he played upon a fellow-operator. Now he would be glad to exchange all his interest in Venango County for one share in the Christian's prospect of heaven. Hopeless, he falls back in his last sickness. His delirium is filled with senseless talk about "percentages" and "commissions" and "buyer, sixty days, " and "stocks up, " and "stocks down. " He thinks that the physician who feels his pulse is trying to steal his "board book. " He starts up at midnight, saying: "One thousand shares of Reading at 116-1/2. Take it! " *Falls back dead. No more dividends.... Swindled out of heaven.* STOCKS DOWN!

LEPROUS NEWSPAPERS.

The newspaper is the great educator of the nineteenth century. There is no force compared with it. It is book, pulpit, platform, forum, all in one. And there is not an interest—religious, literary, commercial, scientific, agricultural, or mechanical—that is not within its grasp. All our churches, and schools, and colleges, and asylums, and art-galleries feel the quaking of the printing-press. I shall try to bring to your parlor-tables the periodicals that are worthy of the Christian fireside, and try to pitch into the gutter of scorn and contempt those newspapers that are not fit for the hand of your child or the vision of your wife.

The institution of newspapers arose in Italy. In Venice the first newspaper was published, and monthly, during the time that Venice was warring against Solyman the Second in Dalmatia. It was printed for the purpose of giving military and commercial information to the Venetians. The first newspaper published in England was in 1588, and called the *English Mercury*. Others were styled the *Weekly Discoverer*, the *Secret Owl*, *Heraclitus Ridens*, etc.

Who can estimate the political, scientific, commercial, and religious revolutions roused up in England for many years past by *Bell's Weekly Dispatch*, the *Standard*, the *Morning Chronicle*, the *Post*, and the *London Times*?

The first attempt at this institution in France was in 1631, by a physician, who published the *News*, for the amusement and health of his patients. The French nation understood fully how to appreciate this power. Napoleon, with his own hand, wrote articles for the press, and so early as in 1829 there were in Paris 169 journals. But in the United States the newspaper has come to unlimited sway. Though in 1775 there were but thirty-seven in the whole country, the number of published journals is now counted by thousands; and to-day—we may as well acknowledge it as not—the religious and secular newspapers are the great *educators of the country*.

In our pulpits we preach to a few hundreds or thousands of people; the newspaper addresses an audience of twenty thousand, fifty thousand, or two hundred thousand. We preach three or four times a week; they every morning or evening of the year. If they are right, they are gloriously right; if they are wrong, they are awfully wrong.

I find no difficulty in accounting for the world's advance. Four centuries ago, in Germany, in courts of justice, men fought with their fists to see who should have the decision of the court; and if the judge's decision was unsatisfactory, then the judge fought with the counsel. Many of the lords could not read the deeds of their own estates. What has made the change?

"Books, " you say.

No, sir! The vast majority of citizens do not read books. Take this audience, or any other promiscuous assemblage, and how many histories have they read? How many treatises on constitutional law, or political economy, or works of science? How many elaborate poems or books of travel? How much of Boyle, or De Tocqueville, Xenophon, or Herodotus, or Percival? Not many!

In the United States, the people would not average one such book a year for each individual!

Whence, then, this intelligence—this capacity to talk about all themes, secular and religious—this acquaintance with science and art—this power to appreciate the beautiful and grand? Next to the Bible, the *newspaper*, —swift-winged, and everywhere present, flying over the fences, shoved under the door, tossed into the counting-house, laid on the work-bench, hawked through the cars! All read it: white and black, German, Irishman, Swiss, Spaniard, American, old and young, good and bad, sick and well, before breakfast and after tea, Monday morning, Saturday night, Sunday and week day!

I now declare that I consider the newspaper to be the grand agency by which the Gospel is to be preached, ignorance cast out, oppression dethroned, crime extirpated, the world raised, heaven rejoiced, and God glorified.

In the clanking of the printing-press, as the sheets fly out, I hear the voice of the Lord Almighty proclaiming to all the dead nations of the earth, —"Lazarus, come forth! " And to the retreating surges of darkness, —"Let there be light! " In many of our city newspapers, professing no more than secular information, there have appeared during the past ten years some of the grandest appeals in behalf of religion, and some of the most effective interpretations of God's government among the nations.

That man has a shrivelled heart who begrudges the five pennies he pays to the newsboy who brings the world to his feet. There are to-day connected with the editorial and reportorial corps of newspaper establishments men of the highest culture and most unimpeachable morality, who are living on the most limited stipends, martyrs to the work to which they feel themselves called. While you sleep in the midnight hours, their pens fly, and their brains ache in preparing the morning intelligence. Many of them go, unrested and unappreciated, their cheeks blanched and their eyes half quenched with midnight work, toward premature graves, to have the "proof-sheet" of their life corrected by Divine mercy, glad at last to escape the perpetual annoyances of a fault-finding public, and the restless, impatient cry for "more copy."

"Nations are to be born in a day. " Will this great inrush come from personal presence of missionary or philanthropist? No. When the time comes for that grand demonstration I think the press in all the earth will make the announcement, and give the call to the nations. As at some telegraphic centre, an operator will send the messages, north and south, and east and west, San Francisco and Heart's Content catching the flash at the same instant; so, standing at some centre to which shall reach all the electric wires that cross the continent and undergird the sea, some one shall, with the forefinger of the right hand, click the instrument that shall thrill through all lands, across all islands, under all seas, through all palaces, into all dungeons, and startle both hemispheres with the news, that in a few moments shall rush out from the ten thousand times ten thousand printing-presses of the earth: "Glory to God in the highest, and on earth peace, good-will toward men! "

You see, therefore, that, in the plain words to be written, I have no grudges to gratify against the newspaper press. Professional men are accustomed to complain of injustice done them, but I take the censure I have sometimes received and place it on one side the scales, and the excessive praise, and place it on the other side, and they balance, and so I consider I have had simple justice. But we are all aware that there is a class of men in towns and cities who send forth a baleful influence from their editorial pens. There are enough bad newspapers weekly poured out into the homes of our country to poison a vast population. In addition to the home manufacture of iniquitous sheets, the mail-bags of other cities come in gorged with abominations. New York scoops up from the sewers of other cities, and adds to its own newspaper filth. And to-night, lying on the tables of this city, or laid away on the shelf, or in the trunk, for more private perusal, are papers the mere mention of the names of which would send a blush to the cheek, and make the decent and Christian world cry out: "God save the city! "

There is a paper published in Boston of outrageous character, and yet there are seven thousand copies of that paper coming weekly to New York for circulation. I will not mention the name, lest some of you should go right away and get it. It is wonderful how quick the fingers of the printer-boy fly, but the fingers of sin and pollution can set up fifty thousand types in an instant. The supply of bad newspapers in New York does not meet the insatiable appetite of our people for refuse, and garbage, and moral swill. We must, therefore, import corrupt weeklies published elsewhere, that make our newspaper stands groan under the burden.

But we need not go abroad. There are papers in New York that long ago came to perfection of shamelessness, and there is no more power in venom and mud and slime to pollute them. They have dashed their iniquities into the face of everything decent and holy. And their work will be seen in the crime and debauchery and the hell of innumerable victims. Their columns are not long and broad enough to record the tragedies of their horrible undoing of immortal men and women.

God, after a while, will hold up these reeking, stenchful, accursed sheets, upon which they spread out their guilt, and the whole universe will cry out for their damnation. See the work of bad newspapers in the false tidings they bring! There are hundreds of men to-day penniless, who were, during the war, hurled from their affluent positions by incorrect accounts of battles that shook the money-market, and the gold gamblers, with their hoofs, trampled these honest men into the mire. And many a window was hoisted at the hour of midnight as the boy shouted: "Extra! Extra! " And the father and mother who had an only son at the front, with trembling hand, and blanched cheek, and sinking heart, read of battles that had never occurred. God pity the father and mother who have a boy at the front when evil tidings come! If an individual makes a false statement, one or twenty persons may be damaged; but a newspaper of large circulation that wilfully makes a misstatement in one day tells fifty thousand falsehoods.

The most stupendous of all lies is a newspaper lie.

A bad newspaper scruples not at any slander. It may be that, to escape the grip of the law, the paragraphs will be nicely worded, so that the suspicion is thrown out and the damage done without any exposure to the law. Year by year, thousands of men are crushed by the ink-roller. An unscrupulous man in the editorial chair may smite as with the wing of a destroying angel. What to him is commercial integrity, or professional reputation, or woman's honor, or home's sanctity? It seems as if he held in his hand a hose with which, while all the harpies of sin were working at the pumps, he splashed the waters of death upon the best interests of society.

The express-train in England halts not to take in water, but between the tracks there is a trough, one-fourth of a mile in length, filled with water; and the engine drops a hose that catches up the water while the train flies. So with bad newspapers that fly along the track of death without pausing a moment, yet scooping up into themselves the pollution of society, and in the awful rush making the earth tremble.

The most abandoned man of the city may go to the bad newspaper and get a slander inserted about the best man. If he cannot do it in any other way, he can by means of an anonymous communication. Now, a man who, to injure another, will write an anonymous letter, is, in the first place, a coward, and, in the second place, a villain. Many of these offensive anonymous letters you see in the bad newspaper have been found to be *written in the editorial chair*.

The bad newspaper stops not at any political outrage. It would arouse a revolution, and empty the hearts of a million brave men in the trenches, rather than not have its own circulation multiply. What to it are the hard-earned laurels of the soldier or the exalted reputation of the statesman? Its editors would, if they dared, blow up the Capitol of the nation if they could only successfully carry off the frieze of one of the corridors. There are enough falsehoods told at any one of our autumnal elections to make the "Father of Lies" disown his monstrous progeny. Now it is the Mayor, then the Governor, now the Secretary of State, and then the President, until the air is so full of misrepresentation that truth is hidden from the view, as beautiful landscapes by the clouds of summer insects blown up from the marshes.

The immoral newspaper stops not at the unclean advertisement. It is so much for so many words, and in such a sheet it will cost no more to advertise the most impure book than the new edition of Pilgrim's Progress. A book such as no decent man would touch was a few months ago advertised in a New York paper, and the getter-up of the book, passing down one of our streets the other day, acknowledged to one of my friends that he had made $18,000 out of the enterprise.

In one column of a paper we see a grand ethical discussion, and in another the droppings of most accursed nastiness. Oh! you cannot by all your religion, in one column, atone for one of your abominations in another! I am rejoiced that some of our papers have addressed those who have proposed to compensate them for bad use of their columns, in the words of Peter to Simon Magus: "Thy money perish with thee! " But I arraign the newspapers that give their columns to corrupt advertising for the nefarious work they are doing. The most polluted plays that ever oozed from the poisonous pen of leprous dramatist have won their deathful power through the medium of newspapers; the evil is stupendous!

O ye reckless souls! get money—though morality dies, and society is dishonored, and God defied, and the doom of the destroyed opens before you—get money! Though the melted gold be poured upon your naked, blistered, and consuming soul—get money! Get money! It will do you good when it begins to eat like a canker! It will solace the pillow of death, and soothe the pangs of an agonized eternity! Though in the game thou dost stake thy soul, and lose it forever—get money!

The bad newspaper hesitates not to assault Christianity and its disciples. With what exhilaration it puts in capitals, that fill one-fourth of a column, the defalcation of some agent of a benevolent society! There is enough meat in such a carcass of reputation to gorge all the carrion-crows of an iniquitous printing-press. They put upon the back of the Church all the inconsistencies of hypocrites—as though a banker were responsible for all the counterfeits upon his institution! They jeer at religion, and lift up their voices until all the caverns of the lost resound with the howl of their derision. They forget that Christianity is the only hope for the world, and that, but for its enlightenment, they would now be like the Hottentots, living in mud hovels, or like the Chinese, eating rats.

What would you think of a wretch who, during a great storm, while the ship was being tossed to and fro on the angry waves, should climb up into the light-house and blow out the light? And what do you think of these men, who, while all the Christian and the glorious institutions of the world are being tossed and driven hither and thither, are trying to climb up and put out the only light of a lost world?

The bad newspaper stops not at publishing the most damaging and unclean story. The only question is: "Will it pay? " And there are scores of men who, day by day, bring into the newspaper offices manuscripts for publication which unite all that is pernicious; and, before the ink is fairly dry, tens of thousands are devouring with avidity the impure issue. Their sensibilities deadened, their sense of right perverted, their purity of thought tarnished, their taste for plain life despoiled—the printing-press, with its iron foot, hath dashed their life out! While I speak, there are many people, with feet on the ottoman, and the gas turned on, looking down on the page, submerged, mind and soul, in the perusal of this God-forsaken periodical literature; and the last Christian mother will have put the hands of the little child under the coverlet for the night, before they will rouse up, as the city clock strikes the hour of midnight, to go death-struck to their prayerless pillows.

One of the proprietors of a great paper in this country gave his advice to a young man then about to start a paper: "If you want to succeed, " said he, "make your paper trashy, intensely trashy, — make it all trash! "

Brilliant advice to a young man just entering business!

It is very often that, as a paper purifies itself, its circulation decreases, and sometimes when a paper becomes positively religious, it becomes bankrupt, unless some benevolent and Christian men come up to sustain it by contributions of money and means. But few religious newspapers in this country are self-supporting. The reason urged is—the country cannot stand so much religion! Hear it! Christian men and philanthropists!

Many papers that are most rapidly increasing to-day are unscrupulous. The facts are momentous and appalling. And I put young men and women and Christian parents and guardians on the look-out. This stuff cannot be handled without pollution. Away with it from parlor, and shop, and store! There is so much newspaper literature that *is* pure, and cheap, and elegant; shove back this leprosy from your door.

Mark it well: *a man is no better than the newspaper he habitually reads.*

You may think it a bold thing thus to arraign an unprincipled printing-press, but I know there are those reading this who will take my counsel; and, in the discharge of my duty to God and man, I defy all the hostilities of earth and hell!

Representatives of the secular and religious press! I thank you, in the name of Christianity and civilization, for the enlightenment of ignorance, the overthrow of iniquity, and the words you have uttered in the cause of God and your country. But I charge you in the name of God, before whom you must account for the tremendous influence you hold in this country, to consecrate yourselves to higher endeavors. You are the men to fight back this invasion of corrupt literature. Lift up your right hand and swear new allegiance to the cause of philanthropy and religion. And when, at last, standing on the plains of judgment, you look out upon the unnumbered throngs over whom you have had influence, may it be found that you were among the mightiest energies that lifted men upon the exalted pathway that leads to the renown of heaven. Better than to have sat in editorial chair, from which, with the finger of type, you decided the destinies of empires, but decided them wrong, that you had been some dungeoned exile, who, by the light of window iron-grated, on scraps of a New Testament leaf, picked up from the hearth, spelled out the story of Him who taketh away the sins of the world.

IN ETERNITY, DIVES IS THE BEGGAR!

THE FATAL TEN-STRIKE.

While among my readers are those who have passed on into the afternoon of life, and the shadows are lengthening, and the sky crimsons with the glow of the setting sun, a large number of them are in early life, and the morning is coming down out of the clear sky upon them, and the bright air is redolent with spring blossoms, and the stream of life, gleaming and glancing, rushes on between flowery banks, making music as it goes. Some of you are engaged in mercantile establishments, as clerks and book-keepers; and your whole life is to be passed in the exciting world of traffic. The sound of busy life stirs you as the drum stirs the fiery war-horse. Others are in the mechanical arts, to hammer and chisel your way through life; and success awaits you. Some are preparing for professional life, and grand opportunities are before you; nay, some of you already have buckled on the armor.

But, whatever your age or calling, the subject of gambling, about which I speak in this chapter, is pertinent.

Some years ago, when an association for the suppression of gambling was organized, an agent of the association came to a prominent citizen and asked him to patronize the society. He said, "No, I can have no interest in such an organization. I am in no wise affected by that evil. "

At that very time his son, who was his partner in business, was one of the heaviest players in "Herne's" famous gaming establishment. Another refused his patronage on the same ground, not knowing that his first book-keeper, though receiving a salary of only a thousand dollars, was losing from fifty to one hundred dollars per night. The president of a railroad company refused to patronize the institution, saying—"That society is good for the defence of merchants, but we railroad people are not injured by this evil; " not knowing that, at that very time, two of his conductors were spending three nights of each week at faro tables in New York. Directly or indirectly, this evil strikes at the whole world.

Gambling is the risking of something more or less valuable in the hope of winning more than you hazard. The instruments of gaming may differ, but the principle is the same. The shuffling and dealing of cards, however full of temptation, is not gambling, unless stakes are put up; while, on the other hand, gambling may be carried on without cards, or dice, or billiards, or a ten-pin alley. The man who bets on horses, on elections, on battles—the man who deals in "fancy" stocks, or conducts a business which extra hazards capital, or goes into transactions without foundation, but dependent upon what men call "luck, " is a gambler.

It is estimated that one-fourth of the business in London is done dishonestly. Whatever you expect to get from your neighbor without offering an equivalent in money or time or skill, is either the product of theft or gaming. Lottery tickets and lottery policies come into the same category. Fairs for the founding of hospitals, schools and churches, conducted on the raffling system, come under the same denomination. Do not, therefore, associate gambling necessarily with any instrument, or game, or time, or place, or think the principle depends upon whether you play for a glass of wine, or one hundred shares in *Camden and Amboy*. Whether you employ faro or billiards, rondo and keno, cards, or bagatelle, the very *idea* of the thing is dishonest; for it professes to bestow upon you a good for which you *give no equivalent*.

This crime is no newborn sprite, but a haggard transgression that comes staggering down under a mantle of curses through many centuries. All nations, barbarous and civilized, have been addicted to it. Before 1838, the French government received revenue from gaming houses. In 1567, England, for the improvement of her harbors, instituted a lottery, to be held at the front door of St. Paul's Cathedral. Four hundred thousand tickets were sold, at ten shillings each. The British Museum and Westminster Bridge were partially built by similar procedures. The ancient Germans would sometimes put up themselves and families as prizes, and suffer themselves to be bound, though stronger than the persons who won them.

But now the laws of the whole civilized world denounce the system. Enactments have been passed, but only partially enforced. The men interested in gaming houses wield such influence, by their numbers and affluence, that the judge, the jury, and the police officer must be bold indeed who would array themselves against these infamous establishments. Within ten years the House of Commons of England has adjourned on "Derby Day" to go out to bet on the races; and in the best circles of society in this country to-day are many hundreds of professedly respectable men who are acknowledged gamblers.

Hundreds of thousands of dollars in this land are every day being won and lost through sheer gambling. Says a traveller through the West—"I have travelled a thousand miles at a time upon the Western waters and seen gambling at every waking moment from the commencement to the termination of the journey. " The Southwest of this country reeks with this abomination. In New Orleans every third or fourth house in many of the streets is a gaming place, and it may be truthfully averred that each and all of our cities are cursed with this evil.

In themselves most of the games employed in gambling are without harm. Billiard-tables are as harmless as tea-tables, and a pack of cards as a pack of letter envelopes, unless stakes be put up. But by their use for gambling purposes they have become significant of an infinity of wretchedness. In New York city there are said to be six thousand houses devoted to this sin; in Philadelphia about four thousand; in Cincinnati about one thousand; at Washington the amount of gaming is beyond calculation. There have been seasons when, by night, Senators, Representatives, and Ministers of Foreign Governments were found engaged in this practice.

Men wishing to gamble will find places just suited to their capacity, not only in the underground oyster-cellar, or at the table back of the curtain, covered with greasy cards, or in the steamboat smoking cabin, where the bloated wretch with rings in his ears deals out his pack, and winks in the unsuspecting traveller, —providing free drinks all around, —but in gilded parlors and amid gorgeous surroundings.

This sin works ruin, first, by unhealthful stimulants. Excitement is pleasurable. Under every sky, and in every age, men have sought it. The Chinaman gets it by smoking his opium; the Persian by chewing hashish; the trapper in a buffalo hunt; the sailor in a squall; the inebriate in the bottle, and the avaricious at the gaming-table.

We must at times have excitement. A thousand voices in our nature demand it. It is right. It is healthful. It is inspiriting. It is a desire God-given. But anything that first gratifies this appetite and hurls it back in a terrific reaction is deplorable and wicked. Look out for the agitation that, like a rough musician, in bringing out the tune, plays so hard he breaks down the instrument!

God never made man strong enough to endure the wear and tear of gambling excitement. No wonder if, after having failed in the game, men have begun to sweep off imaginary gold from the side of the table. The man was sharp enough when he started at the game, but a maniac at the close. At every gaming-table sit on one side Ecstasy, Enthusiasm, Romance—the frenzy of joy; on the other side, Fierceness, Rage, and Tumult. The professional gamester schools himself into apparent quietness. The keepers of gambling rooms are generally fat, rollicking, and obese; but thorough and professional gamblers, in nine cases out of ten, are pale, thin, wheezing, tremulous, and exhausted.

A young man, having suddenly heired a large property, sits at the hazard-table, and takes up in a dice-box the estate won by a father's lifetime sweat, and shakes it, and tosses it away.

Intemperance soon stigmatizes its victim—kicking him out, a slavering fool, into the ditch, or sending him, with the drunkard's hiccough, staggering up the street where his family lives. But gambling does not, in that way, expose its victims. The gambler may be eaten up by the gambler's passion, yet only discover it by the greed in his eyes, the hardness of his features, the nervous restlessness, the threadbare coat, and his embarrassed business. Yet he is on the road to hell, and no preacher's voice, or startling warning, or wife's entreaty, can make him stay for a moment his headlong career. The infernal spell is on him; a giant is aroused within; and though you bind him with cables, they would part like thread; and though you fasten him seven times round with chains, they would snap like rusted wire; and though you piled up in his path, heaven-high, Bibles, tracts and sermons, and on the top should set the cross of the Son of God, over them all the gambler would leap like a roe over the rocks, on his way to perdition.

Again, this sin works ruin by killing industry.

A man used to reaping scores or hundreds of dollars from the gaming-table will not be content with slow work. He will say, "What is the use of trying to make these fifty dollars in my store when I can get five times that in half an hour down at 'Billy's'? " You never knew a confirmed gambler who was industrious. The men given to this vice spend their time not actively employed in the game in idleness, or intoxication, or sleep, or in corrupting new victims. This sin has dulled the carpenter's saw, and cut the band of the factory wheel, sunk the cargo, broken the teeth of the farmer's harrow, and sent a strange lightning to shatter the battery of the philosopher.

The very first idea in gaming is at war with all the industries of society. Any trade or occupation that is of use is ennobling. The street sweeper advances the interests of society by the cleanliness effected. The cat pays for the fragments it eats by clearing the house of vermin. The fly that takes the sweetness from the dregs of the cup compensates by purifying the air and keeping back the pestilence. But the gambler gives not anything for that which he takes.

I recall that sentence. He *does* make a return; but it is disgrace to the man that he fleeces, despair to his heart, ruin to his business, anguish to his wife, shame to his children, and eternal wasting away to his soul. He pays in tears and blood, and agony, and darkness, and woe.

What dull work is ploughing to the farmer, when in the village saloon, in one night, he makes and loses the value of a summer harvest? Who will want to sell tape, and measure nankeen, and cut garments, and weigh sugars, when in a night's game he makes and loses, and makes again, and loses again, the profits of a season?

John Borack was sent as mercantile agent from Bremen to England and this country. After two years his employers mistrusted that all was not right. He was a defaulter for eighty-seven thousand dollars. It was found that he had lost in Lombard street, London, twenty-nine thousand dollars; in Fulton street, New York, ten thousand dollars; and in New Orleans, three thousand dollars. He was imprisoned, but afterwards escaped and went into the gambling profession. He died in a lunatic asylum.

This crime is getting its pry under many a mercantile house in our cities, and before long down will come the great establishment, crushing reputation, home, comfort, and immortal souls. How it diverts and sinks capital may be inferred from some authentic statements before us. The ten gaming-houses that once were authorized in Paris passed through the banks, yearly, three hundred and twenty-five millions of francs! The houses of this kind in Germany yield vast sums to the government. The Hamburg establishment pays to the government treasury forty thousand florins; and Baden Baden one hundred and twenty thousand florins. Each one of the banks in the large gaming-houses of Germany has forty or fifty croupiers standing in its service.

Where does all the money come from? *The whole world is robbed!* What is most sad, there are no consolations for the loss and suffering entailed by gaming. If men fail in lawful business, God pities, and society commiserates; but where in the Bible, or in society, is there any consolation for the gambler? From what tree of the forest oozes there a balm that can soothe the gamester's heart? In that bottle where God keeps the tears of his children, are there any tears of the gambler? Do the winds that come to kiss the faded cheek of sickness, and to cool the heated brow of the laborer, whisper hope and cheer to the emaciated victim of the game of hazard? When an honest man is in trouble, he has sympathy. "Poor fellow! " they say. But do gamblers come to weep at the agonies of the gambler? In Northumberland was one of the finest estates in England. Mr. Porter owned it, and in a year gambled it all away. Having lost the last acre of the estate, he came down from the saloon and got into his carriage; went back; put up his horses, and carriage, and town house, and played. He threw and lost. He started home, and on a side alley met a friend from whom he borrowed ten guineas; went back to the saloon, and before a great while had won twenty thousand pounds. He died at last a beggar in St. Giles. How many gamblers felt sorry for Mr. Porter? Who consoled him on the loss of his estate? What gambler subscribed to put a stone over the poor man's grave? Not one!

Furthermore, this sin is the source of uncounted dishonesties. The game of hazard itself is often a cheat. How many tricks and deceptions in the dealing of the cards! The opponent's hand is ofttimes found out by fraud. Cards are marked so that they may be designated from the back. Expert gamesters have their accomplices, and one wink may decide the game. The dice have been found loaded with platina, so that "doublets" come up every time. These dice are introduced by the gamblers unobserved by the honest men who have come into the play; and this accounts for the fact that ninety-nine out of a hundred who gamble, however wealthy they began, at the end are found to be poor, miserable, ragged wretches, that would not now be allowed to sit on the door-step of the house that they once owned.

In a gaming-house in San Francisco, a young man having just come from the mines deposited a large sum upon the ace, and won twenty-two thousand dollars. But the tide turns. Intense anxiety comes upon the countenances of all. Slowly the cards went forth. Every eye is fixed. Not a sound is heard, until the ace is revealed favorable to the bank. There are shouts of "Foul! Foul! " but the keepers of the table produce their pistols and the uproar is silenced, and the bank has won ninety-five thousand dollars. Do you call this a game of chance? There is no chance about it.

But these dishonesties in the carrying on of the game are nothing when compared with the frauds which are committed in order to get money to go on with the nefarious work. Gambling, with its greedy hand, has snatched away the widow's mite and the portion of the orphans; has sold the daughter's virtue to get means to continue the game; has written the counterfeit signature, emptied the banker's money vault, and wielded the assassin's dagger. There is no depth of meanness to which it will not stoop. There is no cruelty at which it is appalled. There is no warning of God that it will not dare. Merciless, unappeasable, fiercer and wilder it blinds, it hardens, it rends, it blasts, it crushes, it damns. It has peopled Moyamensing, and Auburn, and Sing Sing.

How many railroad agents, and cashiers, and trustees of funds, it has driven to disgrace, incarceration, and suicide! Witness a cashier of the Central Railroad and Banking Company of Georgia, who stole one hundred and three thousand dollars to carry on his gaming practices. Witness the forty thousand dollars stolen from a Brooklyn bank; and the one hundred and eighty thousand dollars taken from a Wall Street Insurance Company for the same purpose! These are only illustrations on a large scale of the robberies *every day* committed for the purpose of carrying out the designs of gamblers. Hundreds of thousands of dollars every year leak out without observation from the merchant's till into the gambling hell.

A man in London keeping one of these gambling houses boasted that he had ruined a nobleman a day; but if all the saloons of this land were to speak out, they might utter a more infamous boast, for they have destroyed a thousand noblemen a year.

Notice also the effect of this crime upon domestic happiness. It hath sent its ruthless ploughshare through hundreds of families, until the wife sat in rags, and the daughters were disgraced, and the sons grew up to the same infamous practices, or took a short cut to destruction across the murderer's scaffold. Home has lost all charms for the gambler. How tame are the children's caresses and a wife's devotion to the gambler! How drearily the fire burns on the domestic hearth! There must be louder laughter, and something to win and something to lose; an excitement to drive the heart faster and fillip the blood and fire the imagination. No home, however bright, can keep back the gamester. The sweet call of love bounds back from his iron soul, and all endearments are consumed in the flame of his passion. The family Bible will go after all other treasures are lost, and if his everlasting crown in heaven were put into his hand he would cry: "Here goes, one more game, my boys! On this one throw I stake my crown of heaven. "

A young man in London, on coming of age, received a fortune of one hundred and twenty thousand dollars, and through gambling in three years was thrown on his mother for support.

An only son went to New Orleans. He was rich, intellectual, and elegant in manners. His parents gave him, on his departure from home, their last blessing. The sharpers got hold of him. They flattered him. They lured him to the gaming-table and let him win almost every time for a good while, and patted him on the back and said, "First-rate player. " But, fully in their grasp, they fleeced him; and his thirty thousand dollars were lost. Last of all he put up his watch and lost that. Then he began to think of home and of his old father and mother, and wrote thus: —

"MY BELOVED PARENTS: —You will doubtless feel a momentary joy at the reception of this letter from the child of your bosom, on whom you have lavished all the favors of your declining years. But should a feeling of joy for a moment spring up in your hearts when you shall have received this from, me, cherish it not. I have fallen deep—never to rise. Those gray hairs that I should have honored and protected I shall bring down with sorrow to the grave. I will not curse my destroyer, but oh! may God avenge the wrongs and impositions practised upon the unwary in a way that shall best please Him. This, my dear parents, is the last letter you will ever receive from me. I humbly pray your forgiveness. It is my dying prayer. Long before you shall have received this letter from me the cold grave will have closed upon me forever. Life is to me insupportable. I cannot, nay, I will not suffer the shame of having ruined you. Forget and forgive is the dying prayer of your unfortunate son. "

The old father came to the post-office, got the letter, and fell to the floor. They thought he was dead at first; but they brushed back the white hair from his brow and fanned him. He had only fainted. I wish he had been dead; for what is life worth to a father after his son is destroyed?

When things go wrong at a gaming-table, they shout "Foul! foul! " Over all the gaming-tables of the world I cry out "Foul! foul! Infinitely foul! "

In modern days, in addition to the other forms of gambling, have come up the thoroughly organized and, in some States, *legalized* institution of lotteries. There are hundreds of citizens on the way to ruin through the lottery system. Some of the finest establishments in town are by this process being demolished, and the whole land feels the exhaustion of this accumulating evil. The wheel of Fortune is the Juggernaut that is crushing out the life of this nation. The records of the Insolvent Court of one city show that, in five years, two hundred thousand dollars were lost by dealing in lottery tickets. All the officers of the celebrated Bank of the United States who failed were found to have expended the money embezzled for lottery tickets.

A man drew in a lottery fifty thousand dollars, sold his ticket for forty-two thousand five hundred dollars, and yet did not have enough to pay the charges against him for lottery tickets. He owed the brokers forty-five thousand dollars.

An editor writes—"A man who, a few years ago, was blest with about twenty thousand dollars (lottery money), yesterday applied to us for ninepence to pay for a night's lodging. "

A highly respectable gentleman drew twenty thousand dollars in a lottery; bought more tickets, and drew again; bought more—drew more largely; then rushed down headlong until he was pronounced by the select men of the village a vagabond, and his children were picked up from the street half starved and almost naked.

A hard-working machinist draws a thousand dollars; thenceforth he is disgusted with work, opens a rum grocery, is utterly debauched, and people go in his store to find him dead, close beside his rum-cask.

It would take a pen plucked from the wing of the destroying angel and dipped in blood to describe this lottery business.

A man committed suicide in New York, and upon his person was found a card of address giving a grog-shop as his boarding house, three blank lottery tickets, and a leaf from *Seneca's Morals*, containing an apology for self-murder.

One lottery in London was followed by the suicide of fifty persons who held unlucky numbers.

There are men now, with lottery tickets in their pocket, which, if they have not sense enough to tear up or throw into the fire, will be their admission ticket at the door of the damned. As the brazen gates swing open they will show their tickets, and pass in and pass down. As the wheel of eternal Fortune turns slowly round, they will find that the doom of those who have despised God and imperilled their souls will be their awful prize.

God forbid that you, my reader, should ever take to yourself the lamentation of the Boston clerk, who, in eight months, had embezzled eighteen thousand dollars from his employer and expended it all in lottery tickets. "I have for the last seven months gone fast down the broad road. There was a time, and that but a few months since, when I was happy, because I was free from debt and care. The moment of the first steps in my downfall was about the middle of last June, when I took a share in a company, bought lottery tickets whereby I was successful in obtaining a share of one-half of the capital prize, since which I have gone for myself. I have lived and dragged out a miserable existence for two or three months past. Oh, that the seven or eight months past of my existence could be blotted out; but I must go, and, ere this paper is read, my spirit has gone to my Maker, to give an account of my misdeeds here, and to receive the eternal sentence for self-destruction and abused confidence. Relatives and friends I have, from whom I do not wish to part under such circumstances, but necessity compels. Oh, wretch! lottery tickets have been thy ruin. But I cannot add more. "

There are multitudes of people who disapprove of ordinary lotteries, yet have been thoroughly deceived by iniquity under a more attractive nomenclature. The lottery in which our most highly respectable and Christian people invest is some "Art Association, " or some benevolent "Gift Enterprise, " in which they fondly believe there can be no harm in drawing Bierstadt's *Yosemite Valley*, or Cropsey's *American Autumn*!

At no time have lottery tickets been sown so broadcast as to-day, notwithstanding the law forbids the old-style lottery.

A few years ago our newspapers flamed with the advertisements of the Crosby Opera House scheme. A citizen of Chicago, finding on his hands an unprofitable building, calls upon the whole country to help him out. Rooms are opened in all the great cities. In rush, not the abandoned and the reprobate (for *they* like the old styles of swindling better), but the educated and refined and polished, until a host of people are in imminent peril of having thrown upon their hands a splendid Opera House. Philadelphia buys thirty thousand dollars worth of tickets. The portentous day approaches. The rail trains from many of the prominent cities bring in dignified"Committees" who come to see that the great abomination is conducted in a decent and Christian manner. The throng presses in. Hold fast your tickets, all you respectable New Yorkers, Philadelphians, and Bostonians, for the wheel begins to move. The long agony is over. Hundreds of thousands of people have made a narrow escape from being ruined by sudden affluence. Swift horses are despatched, that, foam-lathered, dash up to the house of him who owns the successful ticket. The lightnings tell it to the four winds of heaven, and our weekly pictorials hasten forward the photographers to take the picture of the famous man who owned the ticket numbered 58,600. Multitudes think that there has been foul play, and that, after all, they themselves, if the truth were known, did draw the Opera House. Ten years from now there will stand on the scaffold, or behind the prison door, or in the lonely room in which the suicide writes his farewell to wife or parents, men who will say that the first misstep of their life that put them on the wrong road was the ticket they bought in the Crosby Opera House.

The man who won that prize is already dead of his dissipations, and, strange to say, the beautiful building thus raffled away was found to be owned by its original possessor when all the excitement in regard to the matter had died away.

I care not on what street the office was, nor who were the abettors of the undertaking, nor who bought the tickets. I pronounce the whole scheme to have been a swindle, a crime, and an insult to God and the nation.

In this class of gambler-makers I also put the "gift stores, " which are becoming abundant throughout the country. With a book, or knife, or sewing machine, or coat, or carriage there goes a *prize*. At those stores people get something thrown in with their purchase. It may be a gold watch or a set of silver, a ring or a farm. Sharp way to get off unsalable goods. It has filled the land with fictitious articles and covered up our population with brass finger-rings, and despoiled the moral sense of the community, and is fast making us a nation of gamblers.

The Church of God has not seemed willing to allow the world to have all the advantage of these games of chance. A church fair opens, and towards the close it is found that some of the more valuable articles are unsalable. Forthwith the conductors of the enterprise conclude that they will *raffle* for some of the valuable articles, and, under pretence of anxiety to make their minister a present, or please some popular member of the church, fascinating persons are despatched through the room, pencil in hand, to "solicit" shares; or perhaps each draws for his own advantage, and scores of people go home with their trophies, thinking that all is right, for Christian ladies did the embroidery, and Christian men did the raffling, and the proceeds went towards a new communion set. But you may depend on it that, as far as morality is concerned, you might as well have won by the crack of the billiard-ball or the turn of the dice-box.

Some good people cannot stand this raffling, and so, at fairs, they go to "voting, " sometimes for editors, and sometimes for ministers, at a dollar a vote. Now the Methodist minister is ahead; now the Presbyterian leads, and now the Baptist. But, just at the last moment, when one of the ministers of the more popular sect seems sure to get the prize, the members from some obscure denomination, that do not deserve the prize, come in, and by a large contribution carry off for *their* minister the silver tea-set.

Do you wonder that churches built, lighted, or upholstered by such processes as that come to great financial and spiritual decrepitude? The devil says: "*I* helped build that house of worship, and I have as much right there as you have; " and for once the devil is right.

We do not read that they had a lottery for building the church at Corinth or Antioch, or for getting up a gold-headed cane or for an embroidered surplice for Saint Paul. All this I style ecclesiastical gambling. More than one man who is destroyed can say that his first step on the wrong road was when he won something at a church fair.

The gambling spirit has not stopped for any indecency. There lately transpired, in Maryland, a lottery in which people drew for lots in a burying-ground! The modern habit of betting about everything is productive of immense mischief. The most healthful and innocent amusements of yachting and base-ball playing have been the occasion of putting up excited and extravagant wagers. That which to many has been advantageous to body and mind has been to others the means of financial and moral loss. The custom is pernicious in the extreme where scores of men in respectable life give themselves up to betting, now on this boat now on that—now on the Atlantics and now on the Athletics.

Betting, that once was chiefly the accompaniment of the race-course, is fast becoming a national habit, and in some circles any opinion advanced on finance or politics is accosted with the interrogatory"How much will you bet on *that*, sir? "

This custom may make no appeal to slow, lethargic temperaments, but there are in the country tens of thousands of quick, nervous, sanguine, excitable temperaments ready to be acted upon, and their feet will soon take hold on death. For some months and perhaps for years they will linger in the more polite and elegant circle of gamesters, but, after a while, their pathway will come to the fatal plunge. Finding themselves in the rapids, they will try to back out, and, hurled over the brink, they will clutch the side of the boat until their finger-nails, blood-tipped, will pierce the wood, and then, with white cheek and agonized stare, and the horrors of the lost soul lifting the very hair from the scalp, they will plunge down where no grappling hooks can drag them out.

Young man! stand back from all styles of gambling! The end thereof is death. The gamblers enter the ten-pin alley where are husbands, brothers, and fathers. "Put down your thousand dollars all in gold eagles! Let the boy set up the pins at the other end of the alley! Now stand back, and give the gamester full sweep! Roll the first—there! it strikes! and down goes his respectability. Try it again. Roll the second—there! it strikes! and down goes the last feeling of humanity. Try it again. Roll the third—there! it strikes! and down goes his soul forever. It was not so much the pins that fell as the soul! the soul! FATAL TEN-STRIKE FOR ETERNITY! "

Shall I sketch the history of the gambler? Lured by bad company, he finds his way into a place where honest men ought never to go. He sits down to his first game only for pastime and the desire of being thought sociable. The players deal out the cards. They unconsciously play into Satan's hands, who takes all the tricks, and both the players' souls for trumps—he being a sharper at any game. A slight stake is put up just to add interest to the play. Game after game is played. Larger stakes and still larger. They begin to move nervously on their chairs. Their brows lower and eyes flash, until now they who win and they who lose, fired alike with passion, sit with set jaws, and compressed lips, and clenched fists, and eyes like fire-balls that seem starting from their sockets, to see the final turn before it comes; if losing, pale with envy and tremulous with unuttered oaths cast back red-hot upon the heart—or, winning, with hysteric laugh— "Ha! Ha! I have it! I have it! "

A few years have passed, and he is only the wreck of a man. Seating himself at the game ere he throws the first card, he stakes the last relic of his wife, and the marriage-ring which sealed the solemn vows between them. The game is lost, and, staggering back in exhaustion, he dreams. The bright hours of the past mock his agony, and in his dreams, fiends, with eyes of fire and tongues of flame, circle about him with joined hands, to dance and sing their orgies with hellish chorus, chanting—"Hail! brother! " kissing his clammy forehead until their loathsome locks, flowing with serpents, crawl into his bosom and sink their sharp fangs and suck up his life's blood, and coiling around his heart pinch it with chills and shudders unutterable.

Take warning! You are no stronger than tens of thousands who have, by this practice, been overthrown. No young man in our cities can escape being tempted. *Beware of the first beginnings!* This road is a down-grade, and every instant increases the momentum. Launch not upon this treacherous sea. Split hulks strew the beach. Everlasting storms howl up and down, tossing the unwary crafts into the Hell-gate. I speak of what I have seen with my own eyes. I have looked off into the abyss and have seen the foaming, and the hissing, and the whirling of the horrid deep in which the mangled victims writhed, one upon another, and struggled, strangled, blasphemed, and died—the death-stare of eternal despair upon their countenances as the waters gurgled over them.

To a gambler's death-bed there comes no hope. He will probably die alone. His former associates come not nigh his dwelling. When the hour comes, his miserable soul will go out of a miserable life into a miserable eternity. As his poor remains pass the house where he was ruined, old companions may look out a moment and say—"There goes the old carcass—dead at last, " but they will not get up from the table. Let him down now into his grave. Plant no tree to cast its shade there, for the long, deep, eternal gloom that settles there is shadow enough. Plant no "forget-me-nots" or eglantines around the spot, for flowers were not made to grow on such a blasted heath. Visit it not in the sunshine, for that would be mockery, but in the dismal night, when no stars are out, and the spirits of darkness come down horsed on the wind, *then* visit the grave of the gambler!

SOME OF THE CLUB-HOUSES.

Iniquity never gives a fair fight. It springs out from ambush upon the unsuspecting. Of the tens of thousands who have fallen into bad habits, not one deliberately leaped off, but all were caught in some sly trap. You may have watched a panther or a cat about to take its prey. It crouches down, puts its mouth between its paws, and is hardly to be seen in the long grass. So iniquity always crouches down in unexpected shapes, takes aim with unerring eye, and then springs upon you with sudden and terrific leap. In secret places and in unlooked-for shapes it murders the innocent.

Men are gregarious. Cattle in herds. Fish in schools. Birds in flocks. Men in social circles. You may, by the discharge of a gun, scatter a flock of quails, or by the plunge of the anchor send apart the denizens of the sea; but they will gather themselves together again. If you, by some new power, could break the associations in which men now stand, they would again adhere. God meant it so. He has gathered all the flowers and shrubs into associations. You may plant one "forget-me-not" or "hearts-ease" alone, away off upon the hillside, but it will soon hunt up some other "forget-me-not" or"hearts-ease. " Plants love company; you will find them talking to each other in the dew. A galaxy of stars is only a mutual life-insurance company. You sometimes see a man with no out-branchings of sympathy. His nature is cold and hard, like a ship's mast, ice-glazed, which the most agile sailor could never climb. Others have a thousand roots and a thousand branches. Innumerable tendrils climb their hearts, and blossom all the way up; and the fowls of heaven sing in the branches.

In consequence of this tendency, we find men coming together in tribes, in communities, in churches, in societies. Some gather together to cultivate the arts; some to plan for the welfare of the State; some to discuss religious themes; some to kindle their mirth; some to advance their craft. So every active community is divided into associations of artists, of merchants, of bookbinders, of carpenters, of masons, of plasterers, of shipwrights, of plumbers. Do you cry out against it? Then you cry out against a tendency divinely implanted. Your tirades will accomplish no more than if you should preach to a busy ant-hill or bee-hive a long sermon against secret societies.

Here we find in our path the oft-discussed question, whether associations that do their work with closed doors, and admit their members by pass-words, and greet each other with a secret grip, are right or wrong. I answer that it depends entirely upon the nature of the object for which they meet. Is it to pass the hours in revelry, wassail, blasphemy, and obscene talk, or to plot trouble to the State, or to debauch the innocent? Then I say, with an emphasis that no man can mistake, "NO. " But is the object the improvement of the mind, or the enlargement of the heart, or the advancement of art, or the defence of the government, or the extirpation of crime, or the kindling of a pure-hearted sociality? Then I say, with just as much emphasis, "YES. "

There is no need that we who plan for the conquest of right over wrong should publish to all the world our intentions. The general of an army never sends to the opposing troops information as to the coming attack. Shall we who have enlisted in the cause of God and humanity expose our plans to the enemy? No! We will in secret plot the ruin of all the enterprises of Satan and his cohorts. When they expect us by day, we will fall upon them by night. While they are strengthening their left wing, we will double up their right. By a plan of battle formed in secret conclave, we will come suddenly upon them, crying: "The sword of the Lord and of Gideon! "

Secrecy of plot and execution are wrong only when the object and influence are nefarious. Every family is a secret society; every business firm, and every banking and insurance institution. Those men who have no capacity to keep a secret are unfit for positions of trust anywhere. There are thousands of men whose vital need is culturing in capacity to keep a secret. Men talk too much—and women too. There is a time to keep silence, as well as a time to speak. Although not belonging to any of the great secret societies about which there has been so much violent discussion, I have only words of praise for those associations which have for their object the reclamation of inebriates, or like the score of mutual benefit societies, called by different names, that provide temporary relief for widows and orphans, and for men incapacitated by sickness or accident for earning a livelihood.

I suppose there are club-houses in our cities to which men go with clear consciences, and from which they come after an hour or two of intellectual talk, and cheerful interview, to enjoy the domestic circle. But that this is not the character of scores and hundreds of club-houses we all know. Can I, then, pass this subject by without exposition of the monstrous evil? There are multitudes who are unconsciously having their physical, moral, and eternal well-being endangered by club-room dissipation. Was it right to expose the plot of Guy Fawkes, by which he would have destroyed the Parliament of England? And am I wrong in disclosing a peril which threatens not only your well-being here, but your throne in heaven?

I deplore this ruin the more because this style of dissipation is taking down our finest men. The admission-fee sifts out the penurious and takes only those who are called the best fellows. Oh! how changed you are! Not so kind to your wife as you used to be; not so patient with your children. Your conscience is not so much at rest. You laugh more now, and sing louder than once, but are not half so happy. It is not the public drinking-saloon that is taking you down, nor theatrical amusements, nor the houses of sin that have cost thousands of other men their eternity: but it is simply and undeniably your club-room. You do not make yourself as agreeable in your family as once. You go home at twelve o'clock with an unnatural flush upon your cheek and a strange color in your eye that you got at the club. You merely acknowledge that you feel queer. You say that champagne never intoxicates; that it only exhilarates, makes the conversation fluent, shakes up the humor, and has no bad effect except a headache next day. Be not deceived. Champagne may not, like whiskey, throw a man under the table; but if, through anything you drink, you gain an unnatural fluency of speech and glow of feeling, you are simply drunk.

If those imperilled were heartless young men, stingy young men, I would not be so sorry as I am; but there are many of them generous to a fault, frank, honest, cheerful, talented. I begrudge the devil such a prize. After a while these persons will lose all the frankness and honor for which they are now distinguished. Their countenances will get haggard, and instead of looking one in the eye when they talk, they will look down. After a while, when the mother kindly asks,"What kept you out so late? " they will make no answer, or will say "That is my business! " They will come cross and befogged to the store and bank, and ever and anon neglect some duty, and after a while will be dismissed: and then, with nothing to do, will rise in the morning at ten o'clock, cursing the servant because the breakfast is cold, and then go down town and stand on the steps of a fashionable hotel, and criticise the passers-by. While the young man who was a clerk in a cellar has come up to be the first clerk, and he who a few years ago ran errands for the bank has got to be cashier, and thousands of other young men of the city have gone up to higher and more responsible positions, he has been going down, until there he passes through the street with bloated lip, and bloodshot eye, and staggering step, and hat mud-spattered and set sidewise on a shock of greasy hair, the ashes of his cigar dashed upon his cravat. Here he goes! Look at him, all ye pure-hearted young men, and see the work of the fashionable club-room. I knew one such who, after the contaminations of his club-house, leaped out of the third-story window to put an end to his wretchedness.

Many who would not be seen drinking at the bar of a restaurant, think there is no dishonor and no peril connected with sitting down at a marble stand in an elegantly furnished parlor, to which they go with a private key, and where none are present except gentlemen as elegant as themselves. Everything so chaste in the surroundings! Soft carpets, beautiful pictures, cut glass, Italian top tables, frescoed walls. In just such places there are thousands of young men, middle-aged men, and old men, preparing themselves for overthrow.

In many of these club-rooms the talk is not as pure and elevated as it might be. How is it, men and brothers, at half-past eleven o'clock, when the tankards are well emptied, and the smoke curls up from every lip? Do they ever swear? Are there stories told unworthy a man who venerates the name of his mother? Does God, whose presence cannot be hindered by bolt, and who comes in without a pass-word, and is making up His record for the judgment-day, approve of the blasphemies you utter?

You think that there is no special danger, yet acknowledge that you have felt *queer* sometimes. Your head was not right, and your stomach was disturbed. I will tell you what was the matter. *You were drunk.* You understood not that protracted hiccough; it was the drunkard's hiccough. You could not explain that nausea; it was the drunkard's vomit. The fact is that some of you, who have never in your own eyes or in the eyes of others fully sacrificed your respectability, have for six months been written down in God's book as drunkards.

How far down need a man go before he becomes an inebriate? Must he fall into the ditch? No! Must he get into a porter-house fight? No! Must he be senseless in the street? Must he have the delirium tremens? No! He may wear satin and fine linen; he may walk with hat scrupulously brushed; may swing a gold-headed cane, and step in boots of French leather, dismount from a carriage, or draw tight rein over a swift, sleek, high-mettled, full-blooded Arabian span, but yet be so thoroughly under the power of strong drink that he is utterly offensive to his Maker and rotten as a heap of compost.

The fact that this whole land to-day swelters with drunkenness I charge upon the drinking club houses. They wield an influence that makes it respectable, and I will not put my head to the pillow to-night until I have written against them one burning anathema maranatha! When I see them dragging down scores of our young men, and slaying professed Christians at the very altar, and snatching off the garlands of life from those who would otherwise reign forever and forever, I tell you I hate them with a perfect hatred, and pray for more height, and depth, and length, and breadth of capacity with which to hate them.

Along this blossoming and over-arched pathway, and through this long line of temptations that throw their garlands upon the brow, and ring their music into the ear, go a great host.

No one can estimate the homes that have been shattered by the dissipations of the club-house. There are weak women who would never consent to a husband's absence in the evening, however important the duty that takes him away. Any man who wishes to take his share of the public burdens and is willing to work for the political, educational, and social advancement of the community must of necessity spend some of his evenings away from home. There are associations and churches that have a right to demand a share of a man's presence and means, and that is a weak woman who always looks offended when her husband goes out in the evening.

But club-houses become a pest when they demand all a man's evenings; and that is a result we are called to deplore. Every head of a household is called to be its educator, its companion, its religious instructor and exemplar; not only to furnish the wardrobe and to make the money to pay the bills when they come in, but to give his highest intellectual energies and social faculties to the amusement, instruction, and improvement of the household.

But I describe the history of thousands of households when I say that the tea is rapidly taken, and while yet the family linger the father shoves back his chair, has "an engagement, " lights his cigar and starts out, not returning until after midnight. That is the history of three hundred and sixty-five days in the year, except when he is sick and cannot get out.

How about home duties? Have you fulfilled all your vows? Would your wife ever have married you with such a prospect? Wait until your sons get to be sixteen or seventeen years of age, and they too will shove back from the tea-table, have an "engagement, " light their cigars, go over to their club-houses, their night-key rattling in your door after midnight—the effect of your example. And as your son's constitution may not be as strong as yours, and the liquor he drinks more terribly drugged, he will catch up with you on the road to death although you got the start of him. And so you will both go to hell together! A revolving Drummond-light on the front of a locomotive casts its gleam through the darkness as it is turned around; so I catch up the lamp of God's truth and turn it round until its tremendous glare flashes into all the club-houses of our cities.

Flee the presence of the dissipating club-houses. "Paid your money?" Sacrifice that rather than your soul. "Good fellows, " are they? They cannot stay what they are under such influences. Mollusca live two hundred fathoms down in the Norwegian seas. The Siberian stag grows fat on the stunted growth of Altaian peaks. The Hedysarium thrives amid the desolation of Sahara. Tufts of osier and birch grow on the hot lips of volcanic Schneehalten. But good character and a useful life thrive amid club-room dissipations—*Never!*

The best way to make a wild beast cower is to look him in the eye, but the best way to treat the temptations I have described is to turn your back and fly! O! my heart aches! I see men struggling to get out of the serfdom of bad habits, and I want to help them. I have knelt with them and heard their cry for help. I have had them put one hand on each of my shoulders, and look me in the eye, with an agony of earnestness that the judgment shall have no power to make me forget, and from their lips, scorched with the fires of ruin, have heard them cry "God help me! " There is no rescue for such, save in the Lord Almighty.

Well, what we do, we had better do right away. The clock ticks now and we hear it. After a while the clock will tick and we shall not hear it. Seated by a country fireside, I saw the fire kindle, blaze, and go out. I gathered up from the hearth enough for profitable reflections.

Our life is just like the fire on that hearth. We put on fresh fagots, and the fire bursts through and up, and out, gay of flash, gay of crackle—emblem of boyhood. Then the fire reddens into coals. The heat is fiercer; and the more it is stirred, the more it reddens. With sweep of flame it cleaves its way, until all the hearth glows with the intensity—emblem of full manhood. Then comes a whiteness to the coals. The heat lessens. The flickering shadows have died along the wall. The fagots drop apart. The household hover over the expiring embers. The last breath of smoke has been lost in the chimney. Fire is out. Shovel up the white remains. ASHES!

FLASK, BOTTLE, AND DEMIJOHN.

[NOTE. —This chapter, in its first shape, was given some currency under the title of "The Evil Beast. " I have, however, so revised and added to that Lecture, that, as here given, it is essentially a new presentation of the dreadful Abomination of Rum, and it is in this present shape that I wish the public to receive it as a full expression of my views thereon. T.D. W.T.]

There has in all ages and climes been a tendency to the improper use of stimulants. Noah, as if disgusted with the prevalence of water in his time, took to strong drink. By this vice Alexander the Conqueror was conquered. The Romans, at their feasts, fell off their seats with intoxication. Four hundred millions of our race are opium-eaters. India, Turkey, and China have groaned with the desolation; and by it have been quenched such lights as Haller and De Quincey. One hundred millions are the victims of the betel-nut, which has specially accursed the East Indies. Three hundred millions chew hashish, and Persia, Brazil, and Africa suffer the delirium. The Tartars employ murowa; the Mexicans the agave; the people of Guarapo an intoxicating quality taken from sugar-cane; while a great multitude, that no man can number, are the disciples of alcohol. To it they bow. In its trenches they fall. In its awful prison they are incarcerated. On its ghastly holocaust they burn.

Could the muster-roll of this great army be called, and they could come up from the dead, what eye could endure the reeking, festering putrefaction and beastliness! What heart could endure the groans of agony!

Drunkenness: Does it not jingle the burglar's key? Does it not whet the assassin's knife? Does it not cock the highwayman's pistol? Does it not wave the incendiary's torch? Has it not sent the physician reeling into the sick-room; and the minister, with his tongue thick, into the pulpit? Did not an exquisite poet, from the very height of reputation, fall, a gibbering sot, into the gutter, on his way to be married to one of the fairest daughters of New England, and at the very hour when the bride was decking herself for the altar; and did he not die of delirium tremens, almost unattended, in a New York hotel? Tamerlane asked for one hundred and sixty thousand skulls, with which to build a pyramid to his own honor. He got the skulls, and built the pyramid. But if the bones of all those who have fallen as a prey to dissipation could be piled up, it would make a monster pyramid. Talk not of Waterloo and Austerlitz, for they were not fields of blood compared with this great Golgotha.

Who will gird himself for the journey, and try with me to scale this mountain of the dead—going up miles high on human carcasses, to find still other peaks far above, mountain above mountain, white with the bleached bones of drunkards!

Hang not your head or shut your eyes until we have seen it. We must get a sight at the monster before we can shoot him.

I will begin at our national and State capitals. Like government, like people. Henry VIII. blasts all England with his example of uncleanness. Catharine of Russia drags down a whole empire with her nefarious behavior. No Christian man can be indifferent to what every hour of every day goes on at Washington. While the Presidential Impeachment trial advanced, some of the men who were to render their solemn verdict on the subject were reeling in and out of the Senate chamber, —the intoxicated representatives of a free Christian people. It was a great question whether several members of that high court could be got sober in time to vote.

Only recently a Senator from New England rises up with tongue so thick, and with utterance so nonsensical, that he is led into the anteroom. He was a good "Republican. "

One of the Middle States has a representative who very rarely appears in his seat, for the reason that he is so great an inebriate that he can neither walk nor ride. He is a good Democrat.

As God looks down on our State and national legislatures, he holds us responsible. We cast the votes. We lift up the legislators.

Will the time never come when this nation shall rise up higher than partisanship, and cast its suffrage for sober men?

The fact is that the two millions of dollars which the liquor dealers raised for the purpose of swaying State and national legislation has done its work, and the nation is debauched. Higher than legislatures or the Congress of the United States is the Whiskey Ring!

The Sabbath has been sacrificed to the rum traffic. To many of our people the best day of the week is the worst. Bakers must keep their shops closed on the Sabbath. It is dangerous to have loaves of bread going out on Sunday. The shoe-store is closed; severe penalty will attack the man who sells boots on the Sabbath. But down with the window-shutters of the grog shops. Our laws shall confer particular honors upon the rum traffickers. All other traders must stand aside for these. Let our citizens who have disgraced themselves by trading in clothing, and hosiery, and hardware, and lumber, and coal, take off their hats to the rum-seller, elected to particular honor. It is unsafe for any other class of men to be allowed license for Sunday work. But swing out your signs, oh ye traffickers in the peace of families, and in the souls of immortal men! Let the corks fly, and the beer foam, and the rum go tearing down the half-consumed throat of the inebriate. God does not see, does he? Judgment will never come, will it?

People say—"Let us have some law to correct this evil. " We have more law now than we execute. In what city is there a mayoralty that dare do it? There is no advantage in having the law higher than public opinion. What would be the use of the Maine Law in New York? Neal Dow, the Mayor of Portland, came out with a *posse* and threw the rum of the city into the street. From the alms-house a woman came out and said, "Oh! if this had only been done ten years ago, my husband would not have died a drunkard, and I would not have been a widow in the almshouse. "

But there are not enough police in the city of New York to stand by its Mayor in such an undertaking; public opinion is not educated.

I do not know but that God is determined to let drunkards triumph; and the husbands and sons of thousands of our best families be destroyed by this vice, in order that our people, amazed and indignant, may rise up and demand the extermination of this municipal crime.

There is a way of driving down the hoops of a barrel until the hoops break.

We are in this country, at this time, trying to regulate this evil by a tax on whiskey. You might as well try to regulate the Asiatic cholera, or the small-pox, by taxation. The men who distil liquors are, for the most part, unscrupulous; and the higher the tax, the more inducement to illicit distillation. New York produces forty thousand gallons of whiskey every twenty-four hours; and the most of it escapes the tax. The most vigilant officials fail to discover the cellars, and vaults, and sheds where this work is done.

Oh, the folly of trying to restrain an evil by government tariffs! If every gallon of whiskey made, if every flask of wine produced, should be taxed a thousand dollars, it would not be enough to pay for the tears it has wrung out of the eyes of widows and orphans, nor for the blood it has dashed on the altars of the Christian Church, nor for the catastrophe of the millions it has destroyed forever.

Oh! we are a Christian people! From Boston a ship sailed for Africa, with three missionaries, and twenty-two thousand gallons of New-England rum on board. Which will have the most effect: the missionaries, or the rum?

Rum is victor. Some time when you have leisure, just go down any of our streets, and count the number of drinking places. Here they are—first-class hotels. Marble floors. Counter polished. Fine picture hanging over the decanters. Cut glass. Silver water-coolers. Pictured punch-bowls. High-priced liquors. Customers pull off their gloves, and take up the glasses, and click them, and with immaculate pocket handkerchief wipe their mouth, and go up-stairs, or into the reading-room, and complete extensive bargains.

Here it is—the restaurant. All sorts of viands, but chiefly all styles of beverage. They who frequent this place have fairly started on the down grade. Having drunk once, they lounge at the corner of the bar until a friend comes up, and then the beverage is repeated. After a while they sit at the little table by the wall and order a rarer wine; for they feel richer now, and able to get almost anything. Towards bed-time they take out their watch and say they must go home. They start, but cannot stand straight. With a gentleman at each arm, they start up the street. More and more overcome, the man begins to whoop, and shout, and swear, and refuse to go any farther. Hat falls off. Hair gets over his eyes. Door-bell of fine house rings. Wife comes down the stairs. Daughters look over the banisters. Sobbing in the dark hall. Quick—shut the front door, for I do not want to look in. God help them!

Here it is—a wine-cellar. Going into the door are depraved men and lost women. Some stagger. All blaspheme. Men with rings in their ears instead of their nose; and blotches of breast-pin. Pictures on the wall cut out of the *Police Gazette*. A slush of beer on floor and counter. A pistol falls out of a ruffian's pocket. By the gas-light a knife flashes. Low songs. They banter, and jeer, and howl, and vomit. An awful goal, to which hundreds of people better than you have come.

All these different styles of drinking-places are multiplying. They smite a young man's vision at every turn. They pour the stench of their abomination on every wave of air.

I sketch two houses in this street. The first is bright as home can be. The father comes at nightfall, and the children run out to meet him. Luxuriant evening meal, gratulation, and sympathy, and laughter. Music in the parlor. Fine pictures on the wall. Costly books on the stand. Well-clad household. Plenty of everything to make home happy.

House the second. Piano sold yesterday by the sheriff. Wife's furs at pawnbroker's shop. Clock gone. Daughter's jewelry sold to get flour. Carpets gone off the floor. Daughters in faded and patched dresses. Wife sewing for the stores. Little child with an ugly wound on her face, struck in an angry blow. Deep shadow of wretchedness falling in every room. Doorbell rings. Little children hide. Daughters turn pale. Wife holds her breath. Blundering steps in the hall. Door opens. Fiend, brandishing his fist, cries—"Out! Out! What are you doing here! "

Did I call this house the second? No; it is the same house. Rum transformed it. Rum imbruted the man. Rum sold the shawl. Rum tore up the carpets. Rum shook its fist. Rum desolated the hearth. *Rum* changed that paradise into a hell!

I sketch two men that you know very well. The first graduated from one of our literary institutions. His father, mother, brothers and sisters were present to see him graduate. They heard the applauding thunders that greeted his speech. They saw the bouquets tossed to his feet. They saw the degree conferred and the diploma given. He never looked so well. Everybody said, "What a noble brow! What a fine eye! What graceful manners! What brilliant prospects! " All the world opens before him and cries, "Hurrah! Hurrah! "

Man the second. Lies in the station-house to-night. The doctor has just been sent for to bind up the gashes received in a fight. His hair is matted, and makes him look like a wild beast. His lip is bloody and cut.

Who is the battered and bruised wretch that was picked up by the police and carried in drunk, and foul, and bleeding? Did I call him man the second? He is man the *first*! Rum transformed him. Rum destroyed his prospects. Rum disappointed parental expectation. Rum withered those garlands of commencement-day. Rum cut his lip. Rum dashed out his manhood. RUM, accursed RUM!

This foul thing gives one swing to its scythe, and our best merchants fall; their stores are sold, and they slink into dishonored graves.

Again it swings its scythe, and some of our best physicians fall into sufferings that their wisest prescriptions cannot cure.

Again it swings its scythe, and ministers of the gospel fall from the heights of Zion with long-resounding crash of ruin and shame.

Some of your own household have already been shaken. Perhaps you can hardly admit it; but where was your son last night? Where was he Friday night? Where was he Thursday night? Wednesday night? Tuesday night? Monday night?

Nay, have not some of you, in your own bodies, felt the power of this habit? You think that you could stop? Are you sure you could? Go on a little further, and I am sure you cannot. I think, if some of you should try to break away, you would find a chain on the right wrist, and one on the left; one on the right foot, and another on the left. This serpent does not begin to hurt until it has wound around and round. Then it begins to tighten, and strangle, and crush until the bones crack, and the blood trickles, and the eyes start from their sockets, and the mangled wretch cries "O God! O God! Help! Help! " But it is too late; and nothing but the fires of woe can melt the chain when once it is fully fastened.

The child of a drunkard died. My friend, a minister of the Gospel, sat in a carriage with the drunkard, and the coffin of the little child. On the way to the grave, the drunkard put his hand on the lid of his child's coffin and swore that he never would drink again. Before the next morning had come he was dead drunk!

I spread out before you the starvation, the cruelty, the ghastliness, the woes, the terror, the anguish, the perdition of this evil, and then ask, Are you ready, fully and forever, to surrender our churches, our homes, our civilization, our glorious Christianity? One or the other must surrender. It can be no "drawn battle. "

But how are we to contend?

First, by getting our children right on this subject. Let them grow up with an utter aversion to strong drink. Take care how you administer it even as medicine. If you find that they have a natural love for it, as some have, put in a glass of it some horrid stuff and make it utterly nauseous. Teach them as faithfully as you do the catechism, that rum is a fiend. Take them to the alms-house and show them the wreck and ruin it works. Walk with them into the homes that have been scourged by it. If a drunkard hath fallen into a ditch, take them right up where they can see his face, bruised, savage and swollen, and say,"Look, my son: Rum did that! "

Looking out of your window at some one who, intoxicated to madness, goes through the street, brandishing his fist, blaspheming God, —a howling, defying, shouting, reeling, raving and foaming maniac, —say to your son, "Look; that man was once a child like you. " As you go by the grog-shop, let your boy know that that is the place where men are slain, and their wives made paupers, and their children slaves. Hold out to your children all warnings, all rewards, all counsels, lest in after days they break your heart, and curse your gray hairs.

A man laughed at my father for his scrupulous temperance principles, and said—"I am more liberal than you. I always give my children the sugar in the glass after we have been taking a drink. "

Three of his sons have died drunkards; and the fourth is imbecile through intemperate habits.

Again, we will battle this evil at the ballot-box. How many men are there who can rise above the feelings of partisanship, and demand that our officials shall be sober men?

I maintain that the question of sobriety is higher than the question of availability; and that however eminent a man's services may be, if he have habits of intoxication, he is unfit for any office in the gift of a

Christian people. Our laws will be no better than the men who make them.

Spend a few days at Harrisburg, or Albany, or Washington, and you will find out why, upon these subjects, it is impossible to get righteous enactments.

Again, we will war upon this evil by organized societies. The friends of the rum traffic have banded together; annually issue their circulars; raise fabulous sums of money to advance their interests; and by grips, pass-words, signs, and stratagems set at defiance public morals. Let us confront them with organizations just as secret, and, if need be, with grips, and pass-words, and signs maintain our position. There is no need that our philanthropic societies tell all their plans.

I am in favor of all lawful strategy in the carrying on of this conflict. I wish to God we could lay under the wine-casks a train, which, once ignited, would shake the earth with the explosion of this monstrous iniquity.

Again: we will try the power of the pledge. There are thousands of men who have been saved by putting their names to such a document. I know it is laughed at; but there are men who, having once promised a thing, do it. "Some have broken the pledge. " Yes; they were liars. But all men are not liars. I do not say that it is the duty of all persons to make such signature; but I do say that it will be the salvation of many of you.

The glorious work of Theobald Mathew can never be estimated. At his hand four millions of people took the pledge, including eight prelates, and seven hundred of the Roman Catholic clergy. A multitude of them were faithful.

Dr. Justin Edwards said that ten thousand drunkards had been permanently reformed in five years.

Through the great Washingtonian movement in Ohio, sixty thousand took the pledge. In Pennsylvania, twenty-nine thousand. In Kentucky, thirty thousand, and multitudes in all parts of the land. Many of these had been habitual drunkards. One hundred and fifty thousand of them, it is estimated, were permanently reclaimed. Two of these men became foreign ministers; one a governor of a State;

several were sent to Congress. Hartford reported six hundred reformed drunkards; Norwich, seventy-two; Fairfield, fifty; Sheffield, seventy-five. All over the land reformed men were received back into the churches that they had before disgraced; and households were re-established. All up and down the land there were gratulations, and praise to God. The pledge signed, to thousands has been the proclamation of emancipation.

I think that we are coming at last to treat inebriation as it ought to be treated, namely, as an awful disease, self-inflicted, to be sure, but nevertheless a disease. Once fastened upon a man, sermons will not cure him; temperance lectures will not eradicate the taste; religious tracts will not remove it; the Gospel of Christ will not arrest it. Once under the power of this awful thirst, the man is bound to go on; and if the foaming glass were on the other side of perdition, he would wade through the fires of hell to get it. A young man in prison had such a strong thirst for intoxicating liquors, that he cut off his hand at the wrist, called for a bowl of brandy in order to stop the bleeding, thrust his wrist into the bowl, and then drank the contents.

Stand not, when the thirst is on him, between a man and his cups! Clear the track for him! Away with the children: he would tread their life out! Away with the wife: he would dash her to death! Away with the Cross: he would run it down! Away with the Bible: he would tear it up for the winds! Away with heaven: he considers it worthless as a straw! "Give me the drink! Give it to me! Though hands of blood pass up the bowl, and the soul trembles over the pit, —the drink! give it to me! Though it be pale with tears; though the froth of everlasting anguish float in the foam—give it to me! I drink to my wife's woe; to my children's rags; to my eternal banishment from God, and hope, and heaven! Give it to me! the drink! "

Again: we will contend against these evils by trying to persuade the respectable classes of society to the banishment of alcoholic beverages. You who move in elegant and refined associations; you who drink the best liquors; you who never drink until you lose your balance: consider that you have, under God, in your power the redemption of this land from drunkenness. Empty your cellars and wine-closets of the beverage, and then come out and give us your hand, your vote, your prayers, your sympathies. Do that, and I will promise three things: First, That you will find unspeakable happiness in having done your duty; secondly, you will probably save somebody, perhaps your own child; thirdly, you will not, in your last hour, have a regret that you made the sacrifice, if sacrifice it be.

As long as you make drinking respectable, drinking customs will prevail; and the ploughshare of death, drawn by terrible disasters, will go on turning up this whole continent, from end to end, with the long, deep, awful furrow of drunkards' graves.

Oh, how this Rum Fiend would like to go and hang up a skeleton in your beautiful house, so that when you opened the front door to go in you would see it in the hall; and when you sit at your table you would see it hanging from the wall; and when you open your bedroom you would find it stretched upon your pillow; and waking at night you would feel its cold hand passing over your face and pinching at your heart!

There is no home so beautiful but it may be devastated by the awful curse. It throws its jargon into the sweetest harmony. What was it that silenced Sheridan's voice and shattered the golden sceptre with which he swayed parliaments and courts? What foul sprite turned the sweet rhythm of Robert Burns into a tuneless ballad? What brought down the majestic form of one who awed the American Senate with his eloquence, and after a while carried him home dead drunk from the office of Secretary of State? What was it that crippled the noble spirit of one of the heroes of the last war, until the other night, in a drunken fit, he reeled from the deck of a Western steamer and was drowned! There was one whose voice we all loved to hear. He was one of the most classic orators of the century. People wondered why a man of so pure a heart and so excellent a life should have such a sad countenance always. They knew not that his wife was a sot.

"Woe to him that giveth his neighbor drink! " If this curse was proclaimed about the comparatively harmless drinks of olden times, what condemnation must rest upon those who tempt their neighbors when intoxicating liquor means copperas, nux vomica, logwood, opium, sulphuric acid, vitriol, turpentine, and strychnine! "Pure liquors: " pure destruction! Nearly all the genuine champagne made is taken by the courts of Europe. What we get is horrible swill!

I call upon woman for her influence in the matter. Many a man who had reformed and resolved on a life of sobriety has been pitched off into old habits by the delicate hand of her whom he was anxious to please.

Bishop Potter says that a young man who had been reformed sat at a table, and when the wine was passed to him refused to take it. A lady sitting at his side said, "Certainly you will not refuse to take a glass with me? " Again he refused. But when she had derided him for lack of manliness he took the glass and drank it. He took another and another; and putting his fist hard down on the table, said, "Now I drink until I die. " In a few months his ruin was consummated.

I call upon those who are guilty of these indulgences to quit the path of death. O what a change it would make in your home! Do you see how everything there is being desolated! Would you not like to bring back joy to your wife's heart, and have your children come out to meet you with as much confidence as once they showed? Would you not like to rekindle the home lights that long ago were extinguished? It is not too late to change. It may not entirely obliterate from your soul the memory of wasted years and a ruined reputation, nor smooth out from anxious brows the wrinkles which trouble has ploughed. It may not call back unkind words uttered or rough deeds done—for perhaps in those awful moments you struck her! It may not take from your memory the bitter thoughts connected with some little grave: but it is not too late to save yourself and secure for God and your family the remainder of your fast-going life.

But perhaps you have not utterly gone astray. I may address one who may not have quite made up his mind. Let your better nature speak out. You take one side or the other in the war against drunkenness. Have you the courage to put your foot down right, and say to your companions and friends: "I will never drink intoxicating liquor in all my life, nor will I countenance the habit in others. " Have nothing to do with strong drink. It has turned the earth into a place of skulls, and has stood opening the gate to a lost world to let in its victims, until now the door swings no more upon its hinges, but day and night stands wide open to let in the agonized procession of doomed men.

Do I address one whose regular work in life is to administer to this appetite? I beg you—get out of the business. If a woe be pronounced upon the man who gives his neighbor drink, how many woes must be hanging over the man who does this every day, and every hour of the day!

A philanthropist, going up to the counter of a grog-shop, as the proprietor was mixing a drink for a toper standing at the counter, said to the proprietor, "Can you tell me what your business is good for? " The proprietor, with an infernal laugh, said, *"It fattens graveyards! "*

God knows better than you do yourself the number of drinks you have poured out. You keep a list; but a more accurate list has been kept than yours. You may call it Burgundy, Bourbon, Cognac, Heidsick, Hock; God calls it strong drink. Whether you sell it in low oyster cellar or behind the polished counter of first-class hotel, the divine curse is upon you. I tell you plainly that you will meet your customers one day when there will be no counter between you. When your work is done on earth, and you enter the reward of your business, all the souls of the men whom you have destroyed will crowd around you and pour their bitterness into your cup. They will show you their wounds and say, "You made them; " and point to their unquenchable thirst, and say, "You kindled it; " and rattle their chain and say, "You forged it. " Then their united groans will smite your ears; and with the hands out of which you once picked the sixpences and the dimes, they will push you off the verge of great precipices; while, rolling up from beneath, and breaking among the crags of death, will thunder:

"Woe to him that giveth his neighbor drink! "

THE HOUSE OF BLACKNESS OF DARKNESS.

Men like to hear the frailties and faults of others chastised. With what blandness and placidity they sit and hear the religious teacher excoriate the ambition of Ahab, the treachery of Judas, the treason of Athaliah, and the wickedness of the Amalekites. Indeed, I have sometimes felt sorry for the Amalekites, for in all ages, and on all occasions, they are smitten, denounced, and pursued. They have had their full share of censure and excoriation. It is high time that in our addresses in pulpits, and in domestic circles, we turn our attention to the driving out of these worse Amalekites which are swarming in society to-day, thicker than in the olden time. The ancient Amalekites lived for one or two hundred years; but these are not weakened after a thousand years. Those traversed only a few leagues of land; these stalk the earth and ford the sea. Those had each a sword or spear; these fight with a million swords, and strike with a million stings, and smite with a million catastrophes. Those were conquered with human weapons; but to overcome these we must bring out God's great fieldpieces, and employ an enginery that can sweep from eternity to eternity.

There is one subject which we are expected, in all our teachings, to shun, or only to hint at: I mean the wickedness of an impure life. Though God thunders against this appalling iniquity from the heavens curse after curse, anathema after anathema, by our unwillingness to repeat the divine utterance we seem to say, "Lord, not so loud! Speak about everything else; but if this keeps on there will be trouble! " Meanwhile the foundations of social life are being slowly undermined; and many of the upper circles of life have putrefied until they have no more power to rot.

If a fox or a mink come down to the farmyard and carry off a chicken, the whole family join in the search.

If a panther come down into the village and carry off a child, the whole neighborhood go out with clubs and guns to bring it down.

But this monster-crime goes forth, carrying off body and soul; and yet, if we speak, a thousand voices bid us be silent.

I shall try to cut to the vitals of the subject, and proceed with the *post-mortem* of this carcass of death. It is time to speak on this subject. All the indignation of the community upon this subject is hurled upon woman's head. If, in an evil hour, she sacrifice her honor, the whole city goes howling after her. She shall take the whole blame. Out with her from all decent circles! Whip her. Flay her. Bar all the doors of society against her return. Set on her all the blood-hounds. Shove her off precipice after precipice. Push her down. Kick her out! If you see her struggling on the waves, and with her blood-tipped fingers clinging to the verge of respectability, drop a mill-stone on her head.

For a woman's sin, men have no mercy; and the heart of other women is more cruel than death.

For her, in the dark hour of her calamity, the women who, with the same temptation, might have fallen into deeper damnation, have no commiseration and no prayer.

The heaviest stroke that comes down upon a fallen woman's soul is the merciless indignation of her sisters.

If the multitudes of the fallen could be placed in a straight line, it would reach from here to the gates of the lost, and back again.

But what of the destroyer?

We take his arm. We flatter his appearance. We take off our hats. He is admitted to our parlors. For him we cast our votes. For him we speak our eulogies. And when he has gone we read over the heap of compost: "Blessed are the dead who die in the Lord. They rest from their labors and their works do follow them. "

In the fashionable city to-day there walk a thousand libertines. They are a moving pest. Their breath is the sirocco of the desert. Their bones have in them the decay of the pit. They have the eye of a basilisk. They have been soaked in filth, and steeped in uncleanliness, and consumed in sin, and they are all adrip with the loathsomeness of eternal death. I take hold of the robe of one of these elegant gentlemen, and pull it aside, and say, "Behold a Leper! "

First, if you desire to shun this evil, you will have nothing to do with bad books and impure newspapers. With such an affluent literature as is coming forth from our swift-revolving printing-presses, there is no excuse for dragging one's self through sewers of unchastity. Why walk in the ditch, when right beside the ditch is the solid flagging? It seems that in the literature of the day the ten plagues of Egypt have returned, and the frogs and lice have hopped and skipped over our parlor tables.

Waiting impatiently in the house of some parishioner, for the completion of a very protracted toilet, I have picked up a book from the parlor table, and found that every leaf was a scale of leprosy.

Parents are delighted to have their children read, but they should be sure as to what they read. You do not have to walk a day or two in an infected district to get the cholera or typhoid fever; and one wave of moral unhealth will fever and blast an immortal nature. Perhaps, knowing not what you did, you read a bad book. Do you not remember it altogether? Yes; and perhaps you will never get over it.

However strong and exalted your character, *never read a bad book*. By the time you get through the first chapter you will see the drift; If you find the marks of the hoofs of the devil in the pictures, or in the style, or in the plot, away with it. You may tear your coat, or break a vase, and repair them again, but the point where the rip or fracture took place will always be evident. It takes less than an hour to do your heart a damage which no time can entirely repair. Look carefully over your child's library; see what book it is that he reads after he has gone to bed, with the gas turned upon the pillow. Do not always take it for granted that a book is good because it is a Sunday-school book. As far as possible know *who* wrote it, who illustrated it, who published it, who sold it.

Young man, as you value Heaven, never buy a book from one of those men who meet you in the square, and, after looking both ways, to see if the police are watching, shows you a book—very cheap. Have him arrested as you would kill a rattle-snake. Grab him, and shout "Police! police! "

But there is more danger, I think, from many of the family papers, published once a week; in those stories of vice and shame, full of infamous suggestions, going as far as they can without exposing themselves to the clutch of the law. I name none of them; but say that on some fashionable tables there lie "family newspapers" that are the very vomit of the pit.

The way to ruin is cheap. It costs three dollars to go to Philadelphia; six dollars to Boston; thirty-three dollars to Savannah; but, by the purchase of a bad paper for ten cents, you may get a through ticket to hell, by express, with few stopping-places, and the final halting like the tumbling of the lightning train down the draw-bridge at Norwalk—sudden, terrific, deathful, never to rise.

O, the power of an iniquitous pen! If a needle puncture the body at a certain point, life is destroyed; but the pen is a sharper instrument, for with its puncture you may kill the soul. And that very thing many of our acutest minds are to-day doing. Do not think that this which you drain from the glass, because it is sweet, is therefore healthful: some of the worst poisons are pleasant to the taste. The pen which for the time fascinates you may be dipped in the slime of unclean literature.

Look out for the books that come from France. It has sent us some grand histories, poems, and pure novels, but they are few in number compared with the nastiness that it has spewed out upon our shore.

Do we not read in our Bibles that the ancient flood covered all the earth? I would have thought that France had escaped, for it does not seem as if it had ever had a thorough washing.

In the next place, if you would shun an impure life, avoid those who indulge in impure conversation. There are many people whose chief mirthfulness is in that line. They are full of innuendo, and phrases of double meaning, and are always picking out of the conversation of decent men something vilely significant. It is astonishing in company, how many, professing to be *Christians*, will tell vile stories; and that some Christian women, in their own circles, have no hesitation at the same style of talking.

You take a step down hill, when, without resistance, you allow any one to put into your ear a vile innuendo. If, forgetting who you are, any man attempts to say such things in your presence, let your better nature assert itself, look the offender full in the face, and ask—"What do you mean by saying such a thing in my presence! " Better allow a man to smite you in the face than to utter such conversation before you. I do not care who the men or women are that utter impure thoughts; they are guilty of a mighty wrong; and their influence upon our young people is baleful.

If in the club where you associate; if in the social circle where you move, you hear depraved conversation, fly for your life! A man is no better than his talk; and no man can have such interviews without being scarred.

I charge our young men against considering uncleanness more tolerable, because it is sanctioned by the customs, habits, and practices of what is called high life. If this sin wears kid gloves, and patent leathers, and coat of exquisite fit, and carries an opera-glass of costliest material, and lives in a big house, and rides in a splendid turn-out, is it to be any the less reprehended? No! No!

I warn you not so much against the abomination that hides in the lower courts and alleys of the town, as against the more damnable vice that hides behind the white shutters and brownstone fronts of the upper classes.

God, once in a while, hitches up the fiery team of vengeance, and ploughs up the splendid libertinism, and we stand aghast.

Sin, crawling out of the ditch of poverty and shame, has but few temptations; but, gliding through the glittering drawing-room with magnificent robe, it draws the stars of heaven after it.

Poets and painters have represented Satan as horned and hoofed. If I were a poet I should describe him with manners polished to the last perfection, hair flowing in graceful ringlets, eye a little blood-shot, but floating in bewitching languor; hands soft and diamonded; step light and artistic; voice mellow as a flute; boot elegantly shaped; conversation facile, carefully toned, and Frenchy; breath perfumed until it would seem that nothing had ever touched his lips save balm and myrrh. But his heart I would encase with the scales of a monster, then fill with pride, with beastliness of desire, with recklessness, with hypocrisy, with death. Then I would have him touched with some rod of disenchantment until his two eyes would become the cold orbs of the adder; and on his lip would come the foam of raging intoxication; and to his feet the spring of the panther; and his soft hand should become the clammy hand of a wasted skeleton; while suddenly from his heart would burst in crackling and all-devouring fury the unquenchable flames; and in the affected lisp of his tongue would come the hiss of the worm that never dies.

But, until disenchanted, nothing but myrrh, and balm, and ringlet, and diamond, and flute-like voice, and conversation aromatic, facile, and Frenchy.

There are practices in respectable circles, I am told by physicians, which need public reprehension. Herod's massacre of the innocents was as nothing compared with that of millions and millions by what I shall call *ante-natal* murders. You may escape the grip of the law, because the existence of such life was not known by society; but I tell you that at last God will shove down on you the avalanche of his indignation; and though you may not have wielded knife or pistol in your deeds of darkness, yet, in the day when John Wilkes Booth and Antony Probst come to judgment, you will have on *your* brow the brand of *murderer*.

Hear me when I repeat, that the practices of high life ought not to make sin in your eyes seem tolerable. God is no respecter of persons; and robes and rags will stand on the same platform in the day when the archangel, with one foot on the sea and the other on the land, swears, by Him that liveth forever and ever, that Time shall be no more.

O, it is beautiful to see a young man living a life of purity, standing upright where thousands of other young men fall. You will move in honorable circles all your days; and some old friend of your father will meet you and say: "My son, how glad I am to see you look so well. Just like your father, for all the world. I thought you would turn out well when I used to hold you on my knee. Do you ever hear from the old folks? "

After a while you yourself will be old, and lean quite heavily on your cane, and take short steps, and hold the book off to the other side of the light. And men will take off their hats in your presence. Your body, unharmed by early indulgences, will get weaker, only as the sleepy child gets more and more unable to hold up its head, and falls back into its mother's lap: so you shall lay yourself down into the arms of the Christian's tomb, and on the slab that marks the place will be chiseled: "Blessed are the pure in heart, for they shall see God. "

But here is a young man who takes the other route. The voices of uncleanness charm him away. He reads bad books. Lives in vicious circles. Loses the glow from his cheek, the sparkle from his eye, and the purity from his soul. The good shun him. Down he goes, little by little. They who knew him when he came to town, while yet lingering on his head was a pure mother's blessing, and on his lip the dew of a pure sister's kiss, now pass him, and nay, "What an awful wreck! " His eye bleared with frequent carousals. His cheek bruised in the grog-shop fight. His lip swollen with evil indulgences. Look out what you say to him. For a trifle he will take your life. Lower down and lower down, until, outcast of God and man, he lies in the alms-house, a blotch of loathsomeness and pain. Sometimes he calls out for God; and then for more drink. Now he prays; now curses. Now laughs as fiends laugh. Then bites his nails to the quick. Then runs both hands through the shock of hair that hangs about his head—like the mane of a wild beast. Then shivers—until the cot shakes—with unutterable terror. Then, with uplifted fist, fights back the devils, or clutches the serpents that seem winding him in their coil. Then asks for water, which is instantly consumed by his cracked lips. Going his round some morning, the surgeon finds him dead.

Straighten the limbs. You need not try to comb out or shove back the matted locks. Wrap him in a sheet. Put him in a box. Two men will carry it down to the wagon at the door. With chalk, write on the top of the box the name of the exhausted libertine.

Do you know who it is?

That is *you*, O man, if, yielding to the temptations to an impure life, you go out, and perish.

There is a way that seemeth bright, and fair, and beautiful; but the end thereof is BLACKNESS OF DARKNESS FOREVER.

THE GUN THAT KICKS OVER THE MAN WHO SHOOTS IT OFF.

Blasphemy is a crime that aims at God, but does its chief harm to the one that fires it off.

So I compare it to a piece of imperfect firearms to which the marksman puts his eye, and, pulling the trigger, by the rebound finds himself in the dust.

I tell you a story, Oriental and marvellous. History speaks of the richest man in all the East. He had camels, oxen, asses, sheep, and what would make any man rich even if he had nothing else—seven sons and three daughters. It was the custom of this man's children to have family reunions. One day he is at home, thinking of his darling children, who are keeping banquet at their elder brother's house. Yonder comes a messenger in hot haste, evidently, from his looks, bearing evil tidings. Recovering himself sufficiently to speak, he says: "The oxen and the asses have been captured by a foraging party of Sabeans, and all the servants are butchered except myself. " Another messenger is coming. He says that the sheep and the shepherds have been struck by lightning. Another messenger is coming. He says that the Chaldeans have come and captured the camels, and killed all but himself. Another messenger, who says:"While thy sons and daughters were at the feast, a hurricane struck the corner of the tent, and they are all dead! " But his misfortunes are not yet completed. The old man is smitten with the elephantiasis, or black leprosy. Tumors from head to foot; face distorted; forehead ridged with offensive tubercles; eyelashes fall out; nostrils excoriated; voice destroyed; intolerable exhalation from the whole body; until, with none to dress his sores, he sits down in the ashes, with nothing but broken pieces of pottery to use in the surgery of his wounds. At this point, when he needed all consolation and encouragement, his wife comes to him, and says, virtually: "This is intolerable! Our property gone, our children slain, and now this loathsome, disgusting disease is upon you. Why don't you swear? Curse God and die! "

But profanity would not have removed one tumor from his agonized body; would not have brought to his door one of the captured camels; would not have restored any one of the dead children. Swearing would have made the pain more unbearable, the pauperism into which he had plunged more distressing, the bereavement more excruciating.

And yet, from the swearing and blasphemy with which our land is cursed, one would think there were some great advantage to be reaped from the practice. There is to-day in all our land no more prevalent custom, and no more God-defying abomination, than profane swearing. You can hardly walk our streets five minutes without having your ears stung and your sensibilities shocked. The drayman swearing at his horse; the tinman at his solder; the sewing-girl imprecating her tangled thread; the bricklayer cursing at his trowel; the carpenter at his plane; the sailor at the tackling; the merchant at the customer; the customer at the merchant; the printer at the miserable proofsheet; the accountant at the troublesome line of figures; —swearing in the cellar and in the loft, before the counter and behind the counter, in the shop and on the street, in low saloon and fashionable bar-room. Children swear, men swear, ladies (!) swear. Profanity from the lowest haunt calling upon the Almighty, to the fashionable "O Lord! " of the glittering drawing-room.

This whole country is blasted with the evil. Coming from the West, a gentleman sat behind two persons conversing. Profanities were so frequent in the conversation of the two persons in front, that the gentleman behind took out his pencil and paper and made a record. The profanities filled several sheets in the course of two days, at the close of which time the gentleman handed the manuscript to the persons conversing. The men said: "Is it possible that we have uttered so many profanities in the course of two days? " The gentleman said: "Yes. " — "Then, " said one of the men, "I shall never swear again. "

I make no abstract discussion. I hate abstractions. I had rather come right out and have a talk with you about a habit that you admit to be wrong. This habit has grown from the fact that the young often think it an evidence of manliness. There are thousands of boys and youth who indulge in it. I hear children along the street, but just able to walk, practising this iniquity. They cannot talk straight, but they get enough distinctness to let you know that they are damning their own souls and the souls of others. Oh! it is horrible to see a little child, the first time it lifts its feet to walk, set them down on the burning pavement of hell! Between sixteen and twenty years of age there is apt to come a time when a young man is as much ashamed of not being able to deliver an oath as he is of the dizziness that comes from his first cigar. He has his hat and coat and boots of the right pattern, and there is but one thing more now to bring him into *fashion*, and that is a capacity to swear.

So there are some of our young men surrounded by an atmosphere of profanities. Oaths sit on their lips, they roll under their tongues, and nest in the shock of hair. In elegant drawing-rooms they abstain from such utterances, but fill club-room and street with their immoralities of speech. You suggest the wrongfulness of the habit, and they thrust their finger in the sleeve of their vest, and swagger, and say: "Who cares! " They have no regard for God, but great respect for the ladies. Ah! there is no manliness in that.

The most ungentlemanly thing a man can do is to swear. This habit is becoming more and more prevalent because of the immorality of parents and employers. There are very many fathers who indulge in this habit. They feel moved to utter themselves in this way, but first look around to see if their children are present. They have no idea that their children know anything about it. The probability is that if you swear, your children swear. They were in the next room and heard you, or somebody told them about your habit. Your child is practising to do just as you do. He is laughed at, at first, for his awkwardness, but after a while he will swear as well as you.

Then look at the example of master carpenters, masons, roofers, and hatters. You know how some of you go around the building, and, when the work of your journeyman and subordinates does not please you, what do you say? It is not praying, is it? Forthwith, your journeymen and subordinates learn the habit. Hence our hat-shops, and house-scaffoldings, and side-walks, and wharves, and dockyards, and cellars, and lofts ring with blasphemies.

Men argue that, if it is right for a man worth fifty or a hundred thousand dollars to swear, it can be overlooked in men who have merely their day's wages. Because they are poor must they be denied this one luxury?

This habit becomes more prevalent because of the infirmities of temper. There are many men who, when at peace, are most fastidious of speech, but when aroused into the violence of passion, blaze with imprecation. The Oriental's wife spoken of would not have liked her husband to be profane under ordinary circumstances, but now that the camels are gone, and the sheep are gone, and the property is gone, and the boils have come, she says: "Why don't you swear? Curse God and die! " Others, all the year round, have not the froth of profanity wiped from their lips, but try to expend all the fury of a twelvemonth in one red-hot paragraph of five minutes. A man apologized for his occasional swearing by saying that, once in a year, in this way he cleared himself out. There are men who have no control of their blasphemous utterances, who want us to send them to Congress. Others have blasphemed in senatorial places, pretending afterwards that it was a mere rhetorical flourish.

Many fall into this habit through the frequent use of what are called by-words. I suppose that all have favorite phrases of this kind in which there is no harm; but a profusion of this style of speech often ends in bald profanity. It is, "I declare! " "My stars! " "Mercy on me!" "Good gracious! " "By George! " "By Jove! " and "By heavens!" and no harm is intended; but it is a very easy transition from this kind of talk to that which is positively obnoxious. The English language is magnificent, and capable of expressing every shade of feeling and every degree of energy and zeal; and there is no need that we take to ourselves unlawful words. If you are happy, Noah Webster offers to your tongue ten thousand epithets in which you may express your exhilaration; and if you are righteously indignant, there are in his dictionary whole armories of denunciation and scorn, sarcasm and irony, caricature and wrath. Utter yourself against some meanness or hypocrisy in all the blasphemies that ever smoked up from perdition, and I will go on to denounce the same meanness and hypocrisy with a hundred-fold more stress and vehemency in words across which no slime has ever trailed, and through which no infernal fires have shot their forked tongues, —words pure, innocent, all-impressive, God-honored, Anglo-Saxon, —in which Milton sang, and Bunyan dreamed, and Shakespeare wrote.

But whatever be the source of this habit, it is on the increase. At sixteen, boys swear with as much facility as the grandfather did at sixty. Our streets are cursed by it from end to end. Our hotels, from morning until midnight, resound with it. Men curse on the way to the bar to get their morning dram; curse the news-boy who cries the paper; curse the breakfast for being cold; curse at the bank, and curse at the store; curse on the way to bed; curse at the stone against which they strike their foot; and curse at the splinter that gets under the nail. If you do not know that this is so, it is because your ear has been hardened by the perpetual din of profanities that are enough to bring down upon any city the hurricane of fire that consumed Sodom.

The habit is creeping up into the higher circles. Every woman despises flat and unvarnished imprecations; but in the most elevated circles there are women who swear without knowing it. They have read Bulwer, and George Sand, and the exaggerated style of some of our imported as well as home-made periodical literature, until they do not actually know what is decency of speech. With fairy fan to their lips they utter their oaths, and, under chandeliers which discover not the faintest blush, recklessly speak the holiest of names. This is helped on by the second glass of wine, that is *perfectly harmless*; and though no one dare charge her, being so finely dressed, with anything like intoxication, yet there comes a glassiness to the eye, and a glow to the cheek, and a style of speech to the tongue that were not known before she took the second glass that was *perfectly harmless*.

One wild, terrific wave of blasphemy is sweeping over the land. See the effects of this widespread profanity in the increasing perjury. If men in ordinary conversation so commonly use the name of God, is it wonderful that in the jury-box, and in the alderman's office, and in the custom-house so many swear falsely? Notice the way an oath is administered. They toss the Bible at a man, and in the most trivial way say: "So help you God—kiss the book. " I suppose enough lies are every day told in the custom-house to sink it. Smuggling, although it be done against positive oath, is in some circles considered a grand joke; and you say some day to your friend, "How can you sell those goods so cheaply? " and your friend says with an eye-twinkle, "The Custom-House tariff was not as high on those things as it might have been. " Men more easily break their solemn oaths than formerly. What strange verdicts juries do sometimes render! What peculiar charges judges do sometimes make! What unaccountable slowness sheriffs and their deputies sometimes exhibit in the execution of their writs! What erratic railroad enterprises suddenly pass at our State capitals! What wonderful changes Congress makes in the tariff on liquors!

What is an oath? Anything solemn? Anything appealing to the Almighty? Anything stupendous in man's history? No! It is "kissing the book! " In a land where the name of God so often becomes the foot-ball of what are called respectable circles, how can we expect that it can excite any veneration when, in the presence of county clerk, or alderman, or judge, or legislative assembly, it is used in solemn adjuration? This habit lowers, bedwarfs, and destroys the entire moral nature. You might as well expect to raise harvests and vineyards on the side of belching Stromboli as to have any great excellency grow upon your soul when it so often overflows with the scoriæ of this awful propensity. You will never swear yourself up. You will swear yourself down. The Mohammedans, when they find a slip of paper they cannot read, put it aside, for fear the name of God is on it. That, you say, is one extreme. We go to the other.

You are willing to acknowledge this a miserable habit, and would like to have some recipe for its cure.

Reflect much upon the uselessness of the habit. Did a volley of oaths ever start a heavy load? Did curses ever unravel a tangled skein? Did they ever extirpate the meanness of a customer? Did they ever collect a bad debt? Did they ever cure a toothache? Did they ever stop a twinge of the gout? Did they ever save you a dollar, or put you a step forward in any great enterprise? or enable you to gain a position, or to accomplish anything that you ever wanted to do? How much did you ever make by swearing? What, in all the round of a lifetime of profanity, did you ever *gain* by the habit?

Reflect, also, upon the fact that it arouses God's indignation. The Bible reiterates, in paragraph after paragraph, and chapter after chapter, the fact that all swearers and blasphemers are accursed now, and are to be forever miserable. There is no iniquity that has been so often visited with the immediate curse of God.

At New Brunswick, a young man was standing on the railroad track blaspheming. The cars passed, and he was found on the track with his tongue cut out. People could not understand how, with comparatively little bruising of the rest of his body, his tongue could have been cut out. Not long ago, in Chicago, a man told a falsehood, and said that he hoped, if what he said was not true, God would strike him dead. He instantly fell. There was no longer any pulse. There was no reason for his death, except that he asked God to strike him dead, and God did it. In Scotland a club was formed, in which the members competed as to which could use the most horrid oaths. The man who succeeded best in the infamy was made president of the club. His tongue began to swell. It protruded from his mouth. He could not draw it in. He died within three days. Physicians were astounded. There was nothing like it in all the books. What was the matter with him? *He cursed God, and died!* Near Catskill, N.Y., during a thunder-storm, a group of men were standing in a blacksmith-shop. There came a crash of thunder, and the men were startled. One man said that he was not afraid; and he made a wager that he dared go out in front of the shop, while the lightnings were flying, and dare the Almighty. He went out; shook his fist at the heavens, crying,"Strike, if you dare! " Instantly a thunder-bolt struck him. He was dead. He cursed God, and died!

God will not abide this sin. He will not let it escape. There is a kind of manifold paper by which a man may, with a heavy pencil, write upon a dozen sheets at once—the writing going down through all the sheets. So every oath and blasphemy goes through, and is written indelibly on every leaf of God's remembrance. Ah! how much our Father bears! Can you make an estimate of how many blasphemies will roll up from the streets and saloons of our cities to-night? If you go out and look up you cannot see them. There will be no trail of fire on the sky. But the air is full of them. The name of Christ is not so often spoken in worship as in derision. God will be cursed to-night by hundreds of lips. The grog-shops will curse him. The houses of shame will curse him. Five Points will curse him. Bedford street will curse him. Chestnut street will curse him. Madison square will curse him. Beacon street will curse him. Every street in all our cities will curse him.

This blasphemy is an abomination that no words of mine can describe. And God hears it. They curse His name. They curse his Sabbath. They curse his Bible. They curse his people. They curse his Only Begotten Son. Yes; they swear by the name of Jesus! It makes my hair rise, and my flesh creep, and my blood chill, and my breath catch, and my foot halt.

Dionysius had a cave where men were incarcerated. At the top of the cave was an aperture to which he could put his ear, and could hear every sigh, every groan, every word of the inmates. This world is so arranged that all its voices go up to heaven. God puts down his ear and hears every word of praise offered, and every word of blasphemy spoken.

Our cities must come to judgment. All these oaths must be answered for. They die on the air, but they have an eternal echo. Listen for the echo. It rolls back from the ages to come. Listen: —"*All blasphemers shall have their place in the lake that burneth with fire and brimstone.* " Some have thought that a lost soul in the future world will do that which it was most prone to do in this world. If so, then think of a man blaspheming God through all eternity!

116

This habit grows upon a man, until at last it pushes him off forever. I saw a man die with an oath between his teeth. Voltaire rose from his dying pillow, and, supposing that he saw Christ in the room, cried out, "Crush the wretch! " A celebrated officer during the last war fell mortally wounded, and the only word he sent to his wife was: "Tell her I fought like hell! "

There are thousands of men who are having all their moral nature pulled down by the fiery fingers of this habit. At last, pinched, shrivelled, and consumed, they will get down on their beds to die, and at the step of the doctor in the hall, or the shutting of the front door, they will start up, thinking they hear the sepulchral gates creak open.

Who is this God that you should maltreat his name? Has he been haunting you, starving you, or freezing you all your life? No! He is your Father, patient and loving. He rocked your cradle with blessings, from the time you were born. He clothes you now, and always has clothed you. You never had a sickness but he was sorry for you. He has brooded over you with wings of love. He has tried to press you to his heart of kindness and compassion. He wants to forgive you. He wants to help you. He wants to make you happy. He watched last night over your pillow while you slept. He will watch to-night. He was your father's God, and your mother's. He has housed them safe from the blast, and he wants to shelter you. Do you trifle with his name? Do you smite him in the face? Do you thrust him back by your imprecations?

Who is this Jesus Christ that I hear men swearing by? Who is he? Some destroyer, that they so treat his name? What foul thing hath he done, that our great cities speak his name in thousand-voiced jeer and contempt? Who is he? A Lamb, whose blood simmered in the fires of sacrifice, to save you. A Brother, who put down his crown of glory that you might take it up. For many years he has been striving, night and day, to win your affections. There is nothing in heaven that he is not willing to give you. He came with blistered feet and streaming eyes, with aching head and broken heart to relieve you. On the craft of a doomed humanity he pushed out into the sea, to pick you off the rock. Who will ever again malign his name? Is there a hand that will ever again be lifted to wound him? If so, let that hand, blood-dipped, be lifted now. Which one of my readers will ever again utter his sacred name in imprecation? If any, now let them speak. Not one! Not one!

One summer among the New England hills there was an evening memorable for storm and darkness. The clouds, which had been all day gathering, at last unlimbered their batteries. The Housatonic, that flows in silence save as the paddles of pleasure-parties rattle in the row-lock, was lashed into foam and its waves staggered, not knowing where to lay themselves. The hills jarred at the rumbling of God's chariots. Blinding sheets of rain drove the cattle to the bars, and beat against the window-pane as if to dash it in. The corn-fields crouched in the fury, and the ripened grain-fields threw their crowns of gold at the feet of the storm-king. After the night shut in, it was a double night. Its black mantle was rent with the lightnings, and into its locks were twisted the leaves of uprooted oaks, and shreds of canvas torn from the masts of the beached shipping. It was such a night as makes you thank God for shelter, and bids you open the door to let in even the spaniel howling outside with the terror. We went to sleep under the full blast of heaven's great orchestra, and the forests with uplifted voice, in choiring hosts that filled all the side of the mountains, praising the Lord.

We waked not until the fingers of the sunny morn touched our eyelids. We looked out and. Housatonic slept as quiet as a baby's dream. Pillars of white cloud set up along the heavens looked like the castles of the blest, built for hierarchs of heaven on the beach of the azure sea. The trees sparkled as though there had been some great grief in heaven, and each leaf had been God-appointed to catch an angel's tear. It seemed as if God our Father had looked down upon earth, his wayward child, and stooped to her tear-wet cheek, and kissed it.

Even so will the darkness of our country's crime and suffering be lifted. God will roll back the night of storm, and bring in the morning of joy. Its golden light will gild the city spire, and strike the forests of Maine, and tinge the masts of Mobile; and with one end resting upon the Atlantic beach and the other on the Pacific coast, God will spring a great rainbow arch of peace, in token of everlasting covenant that the land shall never again be deluged with crime.

LIES: WHITE AND BLACK.

There are ten thousand ways of telling a lie. A man's entire life may be a falsehood, while with his lips he may not once directly falsify. There are those who state what is positively untrue, but afterwards say, "may be, " softly. These departures from the truth are called"white lies; " but there is really no such thing as a white lie. The whitest lie that was ever told was as black as perdition. No inventory of public crimes will be sufficient that omits this gigantic abomination. There are men, high in Church and State, actually useful, self-denying, and honest in many things, who, upon certain subjects, and in certain spheres, are not at all to be depended upon for veracity. Indeed, there are multitudes of men who have their notions of truthfulness so thoroughly perverted, that they do not know when they *are* lying. With many it is a cultivated sin; with some it seems a natural infirmity. I have known people who seemed to have been born liars. The falsehoods of their lives extended from cradle to grave. Prevarication, misrepresentation, and dishonesty of speech appeared in their first utterances and was as natural to them as any of their infantile diseases, and was a sort of moral croup or spiritual scarlatina. But many have been placed in circumstances where this tendency has day by day, and hour by hour, been called to larger development. They have gone from attainment to attainment, and from class to class, until they have become regularly graduated liars.

The air of the city is filled with falsehoods. They hang pendent from the chandeliers of our finest residences; they crowd the shelves of some of our merchant princes; they fill the side-walk from curb-stone to brown-stone facing. They cluster around the mechanic's hammer, and blossom from the end of the merchant's yard-stick, and sit in the doors of churches. Some call them "fiction. " Some style them"fabrication. " You might say that they were subterfuge, disguise, delusion, romance, evasion, pretence, fable, deception, misrepresentation; but, as I am ignorant of anything to be gained by the hiding of a God-defying outrage under a lexicographer's blanket, I shall chiefly call them what my father taught me to call them—*lies.*

I shall divide them into agricultural, mercantile, mechanical, and ecclesiastical lies; leaving those that are professional, social, and political for some other chapter.

First, then, I will speak of those that are more particularly *agricultural*. There is something in the perpetual presence of natural objects to make a man pure. The trees never issue "false stock. " Wheat-fields are always honest. Rye and oats never move out in the night, not paying for the place they have occupied. Corn shocks never make false assignments. Mountain brooks are always"current." The gold on the grain is never counterfeit. The sunrise never flaunts in false colors. The dew sports only genuine diamonds.

Taking farmers as a class, I believe they are truthful, and fair in dealing, and kind-hearted. But the regions surrounding our cities do not always send this sort of men to our markets. Day by day there creak through our streets, and about the market-houses, farm wagons that have not an honest spoke in their wheels, or a truthful rivet from tongue to tail-board. During the last few years there have been times when domestic economy has foundered on the farmer's firkin. Neither high taxes, nor the high price of dry-goods, nor the exorbitancy of labor, could excuse much that the city has witnessed in the behavior of the yeomanry. By the quiet firesides of Westchester and Bucks counties I hope there may be seasons of deep reflection and hearty repentance.

Rural districts are accustomed to rail at great cities as given up to fraud and every form of unrighteousness; but our cities do not absorb all the abominations. Our citizens have learned the importance of not always trusting to the size and style of apples in the top of a farmer's barrel, as an indication of what may be found farther down. Many of our people are accustomed to watch to see how correctly a bushel of beets is measured; and there are not many honest milk-cans. Deceptions do not all cluster around city halls. When our cities sit down and weep over their sins, all the surrounding counties ought to come in and weep with them.

There is often hostility on the part of producers against traders, as though the man who raises the corn were necessarily more honorable than the grain dealer, who pours it into his mammoth bin. There ought to be no such hostility. The occupation of one is as necessary as that of the other. Yet producers often think it no wrong to snatch away from the trader; and they say to the bargain-maker,"You get your money easy. " Do they get it easy? Let those who in the quiet field and barn get their living exchange places with those who stand to-day amid the excitements of commercial life, and see if they find it so very easy. While the farmer goes to sleep with the assurance that his corn and barley will be growing all the night, moment by moment adding to his revenue, the merchant tries to go to sleep, conscious that that moment his cargo may be broken on the rocks, or damaged by the wave that sweeps clear across the hurricane deck; or that the gold gamblers may, that very hour, be plotting some monetary revolution, or the burglars be prying open his safe, or his debtors fleeing the town, or his landlord raising the rent, or the fires kindling on the block that contains all his estate. *Easy!* is it? God help the merchants! It is hard to have the palms of the hand blistered with out-door work; but a more dreadful process when, through mercantile anxieties, the brain is consumed!

In the next place we notice *mercantile* lies, those before the counter and behind the counter. I will not attempt to specify the different forms of commercial falsehood. There are merchants who excuse themselves for deviation from truthfulness because of what they call commercial custom. In other words, the multiplication and universality of a sin turns it into a virtue. There have been large fortunes gathered where there was not one drop of unrequited toil in the wine; not one spark of bad temper flashing from the bronze bracket; not one drop of needle-woman's heart-blood in the crimson plush; while there are other great establishments in which there is not one door-knob, not one brick, not one trinket, not one thread of lace, but has upon it the mark of dishonor. What wonder if, some day, a hand of toil that had been wrung, and worn out, and blistered until the skin came off, should be placed against the elegant wall-paper, leaving its mark of blood, —four fingers and a thumb; or that, some day, walking the halls, there should be a voice accosting the occupant, saying, *Six cents for making a shirt*; and, flying the room, another voice should say, *Twelve cents for an army blanket*; and the man should try to sleep at night, but ever and anon be aroused, until, getting up on one elbow, he should shriek out, *Who's there?*

There are thousands of fortunes made in commercial spheres that are throughout righteous. God will let his favor rest upon every scroll, every pictured wall, every traceried window; and the joy that flashes from the lights, and showers from the music, and dances in the children's quick feet, pattering through the hall, will utter the congratulation of men and the approval of God.

A merchant can, to the last item, be thoroughly honest. There is never any need of falsehood. Yet how many will, day by day, hour by hour, utter what they *know* to be wrong. You say that you are selling at less than cost. If so, then it is right to say it. But did that thing cost you less than what you ask for it? If not, then you have lied. You say that article cost you twenty-five dollars. Did it? If so, then all right. If it did not, then you have lied. Suppose you are a purchaser. You are "beating down" the goods. You say that that article, for which five dollars is charged, is not worth more than four. Is it worth no more than four dollars? Then all right. If it be worth more, and, for the sake of getting it for less than its value, you wilfully depreciate it, you have lied. *You* may call it a sharp trade. The recording angel writes it down on the ponderous tomes of eternity—"Mr. So and So, merchant on Water street, or in Eighth street, or in State street; or Mrs. So and So, keeping house on Beacon street, or on Madison avenue, or Rittenhouse square, told one lie. " You may consider it insignificant, because relating to an insignificant purchase. You would despise the man who would falsify in regard to some great matter, in which the city or the whole country was concerned; but this is only a box of buttons, or a row of pins, or a case of needles. Be not deceived. The article purchased may be so small you can put it in your vest pocket, but the sin was bigger than the Pyramids, and the echo of the dishonor will reverberate through all the mountains of eternity.

You throw out on your counter some specimens of handkerchiefs. Your customer asks, "Is that all silk? no cotton in it? " You answer,"It is all silk. " Was it all silk? If so, all right. But was it partly cotton? Then you have lied. Moreover, you lost by the falsehood. The customer, though he may live at Lynn, or Doylestown, or Poughkeepsie, will find out that you defrauded him, and next spring, when he again comes shopping, he will look at your sign and say: "I will not try there. That is the place where I got that handkerchief. " So that, by that one dishonest bargain, you picked your own pocket and insulted the Almighty.

Would you dare to make an estimate of how many falsehoods in trade were yesterday told by hardware men, and clothiers, and fruit-dealers, and dry-goods establishments, and importers, and jewellers, and lumbermen, and coal-merchants, and stationers, and tobacconists? Lies about saddles, about buckles, about ribbons, about carpets, about gloves, about coats, about shoes, about hats, about watches, about carriages, about books, —about everything. In the name of the Lord Almighty, I arraign commercial falsehoods as one of the greatest of abominations in city and town.

In the next place, I notice *mechanical* lies. There is no class of men who administer more to the welfare of the city than artisans. To their hand we must look for the building that shelters us, for the garments that clothe us, for the car that carries us. They wield a widespread influence. There is much derision of what is called *"muscular Christianity; "* but in the latter day of the world's prosperity, I think that the Christian will be muscular. We have the right to expect of those stalwart men of toil the highest possible integrity. Many of them answer all our expectations, and stand at the front of religious and philanthropic enterprises. But this class, like the others that I have named, has in it those who lack in the element of veracity. They cannot all be trusted. In times when the demand for labor is great, it is impossible to meet the demands of the public, or do work with that promptness and perfection that would at other times be possible. But there are mechanics whose word cannot be trusted at any time. No man has a right to promise more work than he can do. There are mechanics who say that they will come Monday, but they do not come until Wednesday. You put work in their hands that they tell you shall be completed in ten days, but it is thirty. There have been houses built of which it might be said that every nail driven, every foot of plastering put on, every yard of pipe laid, every shingle hammered, every brick mortared, could tell of falsehood connected therewith. There are men attempting to do ten or fifteen pieces of work who have not the time or strength to do more than five or six pieces; but by promises never fulfilled keep all the undertakings within their own grasp. This is what they call *"nursing" the job*.

How much wrong to his soul and insult to God a mechanic would save, if he promised only so much as he expected to be able to do. Society has no right to ask of you impossibilities.

You cannot always calculate correctly, and you may fail because you cannot get the help that you anticipate. But now I am speaking of the wilful making of promises that you know you cannot keep. Did you say that that shoe should be mended, that coat repaired, those brick laid, that harness sewed, that door grained, that spout fixed, or that window glazed, by Saturday, knowing that you would neither be able to do it yourself nor get any one else to do it? Then, before God and man, you are a liar. You may say that it makes no particular difference, and that if you had told the truth you would have lost the job, and that people expect to be disappointed. But that excuse will not answer. There is a voice of thunder rolling among the drills, and planes, and shoe-lasts, and shears, which says: "All liars shall have their place in the lake that burneth with fire and brimstone. "

I next notice *ecclesiastical* lies; that is, falsehoods told for the purpose of advancing churches and sects, or for the purpose of depleting them. There is no use in asking many a Calvinist what an Arminian believes, for he will be apt to tell you that the Arminian believes that a man can convert himself; or to ask the Arminian what the Calvinist believes, for he will tell you that the Calvinist believes that God made some men just to damn them. There is no need of asking a pedo-Baptist what a Baptist believes, for he will be apt to say that the Baptist believes immersion to be positively necessary to salvation. It is almost impossible for one denomination of Christians, without prejudice or misrepresentation, to state the sentiment of an opposing sect. If a man hates Presbyterians, and you ask him what Presbyterians believe, he will tell you that they believe that there are infants in hell a span long.

It is strange also how individual churches will sometimes make misstatements about other individual churches. It is especially so in regard to falsehoods told with reference to prosperous enterprises. As long as a church is feeble, and the singing is discordant, and the minister, through the poverty of the church, must go with threadbare coat, and here and there a worshipper sits in the end of a pew having all the seat to himself, religious sympathizers of other churches will say, "What a pity! " But, let a great day of prosperity come, and even ministers of the gospel, who ought to be rejoiced at the largeness and extent of the work, denounce, and misrepresent, and falsify, —starting the suspicion, in regard to themselves, that the reason they do not like the corn is because it is not ground in their own mill.

How long before we shall learn to be fair in our religious criticisms! The keenest jealousies on earth are church jealousies. The field of Christian work is so large that there is no need that our hoe-handles hit.

May God extirpate from the world ecclesiastical lies, commercial lies, mechanical lies, and agricultural lies, and make every man, the world over, to speak truth with his neighbor!

A GOOD TIME COMING.

As on some bitter cold night, while threshing our hands about to keep our thumbs from freezing, we have looked up and seen the northern lights blazing along the sky, the windows of heaven illumined at the news of some great victory, so from beyond this bitter night of abomination a brightness strikes through from the other side.

I have thought that it would be well, in these chapters on the sins of the times, to lift before you a vision of what our cities will be when the work of good men shall have been concluded and our population redeemed. I doubt not that sometimes men have shut this book, thinking that the gigantic wrongs we depict may never be discomfited. Lest you be utterly disheartened, I will show you that we fight in a war in which we will be completely victorious. This is to be no drawn battle; for, when it is done, the result will not be disputed by a man on earth, or an angel in heaven, or a devil in hell. We shall have captured every one of the strongholds of darkness. You and I will live to see the day when gambling-hells will be changed into places of Christian merchandise, and houses of sin swept and garnished for the residence of the purest home circles.

Beethoven was deaf, and could not hear the airs he composed; but when the song of universal disenthralment arises, and white Circassian stands up by the side of black Ethiopian, and tropical groves wave to the Lebanon cedars, we shall, standing somewhere, know it and see it, and hear it. If gone from earth, we will be allowed to come out on the hills and look.

We do not talk about impossibilities. We do not propose a medicine about which we have to say that it will "kill or cure. " For this balm that oozes from the tree of heaven will inevitably cure.

I remark that this coming time of municipal elevation will be a time of financial prosperity. Many seem to suppose that when the world's better days come, the people will forsake their industries, and give themselves to perpetual psalm-singing, and, being all absorbed in spiritual things, will become reckless as to dress and dwelling; and very rigid laws then governing the commercial world, all enterprise and speculation will cease, and all hilarity be stricken out of the social circle. There is no warrant for such an absurd anticipation. I suppose that when society is reconstructed, where there is now, in the course of a year, one fortune made, there will be a hundred fortunes made. Every one knows that the commercial world thrives in proportion as there is confidence between man and man; and the extirpation of all double-dealing and fraud from society will increase this confidence, and hence greater prosperity. The heavy commercial disasters that have smitten this land were the work of godless speculators and infamous stock-gamblers. It is crime that is the mightiest foe to business; but when the right shall hurl back into ruin the plots of bad men, and purify the commercial code, and thunder down fraudulent establishments, and put into the hands of honest men the keys of commercial prosperity, blessed will be the bargain-makers of the city.

That will be a prosperous time, for taxes will be a mere nothing. Every style of business is taxed now to the utmost. City taxes, county taxes, State taxes, United States taxes, license taxes, manufacturing taxes, stamp taxes, —taxes! taxes! taxes! Our citizens must make a small fortune every year to meet these exactions. What hand fastens to all of our great industries this tremendous load? Crime! We have to pay the board of every man and woman who, by intemperance, is cast into the alms-house. We have to support the orphans of those who plunge themselves into their graves by beastly indulgences. We support from our pockets the large machinery of municipal government, which is vast just in proportion as the criminal proclivities of the city are great. What makes necessary hospitals, houses of refuge, police-stations, and alms-houses, the Tombs, Sing Sing, and Moyamensing?

In that good time coming there shall be no exhaustive taxation; no orphans homeless, for parents will be able to leave their children a competency; no prisons, for crime will have given place to virtue. Then the vast swindles which now, from time to time, disgrace our cities, will be unheard of. No voting of public money that, on its way to some city improvement, falls into the pockets of those who voted it. No courts of Oyer and Terminer, at vast expense to the people. No empanelling of juries to inquire into theft, arson, murder, slander, and black-mail. In that day of redemption there will be better factories, grander architecture, finer equipages, larger estates, richer opulence.

Again: when our cities are purified the churches will be multiplied, purified, and strengthened. Now, denominations, and the individuals of the different sects, are often jealous of each other. Christians are not always kindly disposed toward each other; and ministers of the gospel sometimes forget the bond of brotherhood. In that day they will be sympathetic and helpful. There may be differences of opinion and sentiment, but no acerbity, no hypercriticism, and no exclusiveness. In that day all the churches will be filled with worshippers. We have not to-day, in the cities, church-room for one-fourth of our population; and yet there is a great deal more room than the people occupy. The churches do not average an attendance of five hundred people. The vast majority do not attend public worship. But in the day of which I speak there will be enough church-room to hold all the people, and the room will be occupied. In that time what rousing songs will be sung! What earnest sermons will be preached! What fervent prayers will be offered! In these days a *fashionable* church is a place where, after a careful toilet, a few people come in, sit down, and what time they can get their minds off their stores, or away from the new style of hat in the seat before them, listen in silence to the minister—warranted to hit no man's sins—and to the choir, who are agreed to sing tunes that nobody knows; and, having passed away an hour in dreamy lounging, go home refreshed.

I pronounce much of what is called "church music, " in our day, a mockery and a farce. Though I have neither a cultured voice nor a cultured ear, no man shall do my singing. When the storms, and the trees, and the dragons are called on to praise the Lord, I feel that I must sing, for I know more about music than do the dragons. Nothing can take the place of artistic music. The dollar that I pay to hear Parepa or Nilsson sing is far from being wasted. But, when the hymn is read, and the angels of God stoop from their thrones to bear up on their wings the praise of the great congregation, let us not drive them away with our indifference. I have preached in churches where fabulous sums of money were paid to performers, and the harmony was exquisite as any harmony that ever went up from an Academy of Music; and yet, for all the purposes of devotion, I would prefer the hearty, out-breaking song of a backwoods Methodist camp-meeting. When these fancy starveling songs get up to the gate of heaven, how do you suppose they look, standing beside the great doxologies of the glorified? Let an operatic performance, floating upward, get many hours the start, and it shall be caught and passed by the shout of the Sailors' Bethel, or the hosanna of the Sabbath-school children.

I know a church where there was no singing except that done by the choir, save one old Christian man; and they waited upon him by a committee, and asked him if he would not stop singing, for he disturbed the choir!

The day cometh when all the churches will rejoice in this department of service, rightly conducted, and when from all the great audiences of attentive worshippers will rise a multitudinous anthem.

"O God! let all the people praise thee! " Again: when the city is redeemed, the low haunts of vice and pollution will be extinguished. Mr. Etzler, of England, proposes, by the forces of tide, and wind, and wave, and sunshine, to reconstruct the world. In a book of much genius, which rushed rapidly from edition to edition, he says: — "Fellow-men: I promised to show the means of creating a paradise within ten years, where everything desirable for human life may be had by every man in superabundance, without labor and without pay; where the whole face of nature shall be changed into the most beautiful forms, and man may live in the most magnificent palaces, in all imaginable refinements of luxury, and in the most delightful gardens; where he may accomplish without labor, in one year, more than hitherto could be done in thousands of years; may level continents; sink valleys; create lakes; drain lakes and swamps, and intersect the land everywhere with beautiful canals and roads for transporting heavy loads of many thousand tons, and for travelling a thousand miles in twenty-four hours; may cover the ocean with floating islands, movable in any desired direction, with an immense power and celerity, in perfect security, and with all the comforts and luxuries; bearing gardens and palaces, with thousands of families, and provided with rivulets of sweet water; may explore the interior of the globe, and travel from pole to pole in a fortnight; provide himself with means yet unheard of for increasing his knowledge of the world, and so his intelligence; leading a life of continual happiness, of enjoyment yet unknown; free himself from almost all the evils that afflict mankind except death, and even put death far beyond the common period of human life, and, finally, render it less afflicting. From the houses to be built will be afforded the most enrapturing views to be fancied; from the galleries, from the roof, and from its turrets may be seen gardens, as far as the eye can see, full of fruits and flowers, arranged in the most beautiful order, with walks, colonnades, aqueducts, canals, ponds, plains, amphitheatres, terraces, fountains, sculptured works, pavilions, gondolas, places for public amusement, to delight the eye and fancy. All this to be done by urging the water, the wind, and the sunshine to their full development. " Mr. Etzler gives plates of the machinery by which all this is to be done. He proposes the organization of a company; and says small shares of twenty dollars will be sufficient—in all from two hundred thousand to three hundred thousand dollars—to create the first establishment for a whole community, of from three to four thousand individuals. "At the end of five years we shall have a principal of two hundred millions of dollars; and so paradise will be wholly regained at the end of the tenth year. "

There is more reason in this than in many of the plans proposed; but mechanical forces can never recreate the world. I shall take no shares in the large company that is proposed; my faith is that Christianity will yet make the worst street of our cities better than the best street now is.

Archimedes consumed the enemies of Syracuse by a great sun-glass. As the ships came up the harbor, the sun's rays were concentrated upon them: now the sails are wings of fire; the masts fall, and the vessels sink. So, by the great sun-glass of the Gospel, the rays of heaven will be concentred upon all the filth and unchastity and crime of our great towns, and under the heat they will blaze and expire. When the day comes that I have shown will come, suppose you that there will be any midnight brawls? any shivering mendicants, kicked off from the marble steps? any droves of unwashed, uncombed, unfed children? any blasphemers in the street? any staggering past of inebriates? No! No wine-cellars. No lager-beer saloons. No distilleries where they make the XXX. No bloated cheeks. No blood-shot eyes. No fist-battered foreheads. The grandchildren of that woman who now walks up the street with a curse, as the boys stone her, will be philanthropists, and heal the sick, and manage great commercial enterprises.

When our cities are so raised, we shall have a different style of municipal government. The great question, in regard to the execution of the law, now is: "What is popular? " Our city governments slumber—great carcasses of insufficiency, sending up their stench into the nostrils of high heaven, while there are thousands of gambling-houses, and drinking-saloons, and more places of damnable lust than the decency of the country has time to count. Do you tell me that the authorities do not know it? They do know it. All the police know it. The sheriff and his deputies know it. The aldermen know it. The mayors know it. Everybody who keeps his eyes and ears open knows it. In the name of God I impeach the municipal authorities of many of our cities, that they neglect to execute the law. You cannot charge it upon any one party. Within the past few years both parties, and all kinds of parties, have been in power; but the work has never been done. You have but to pass the City Hall, or look in upon the rooms of some of our city officials, to see to what sort of men our cities have been abandoned. Look at the swearing, bloated, sensual wretches who stand on the outside of the New York City Hall, picking their teeth, waiting for some crumbs of emolument to fall at their feet; and then tell me how far it is from New York to Sodom. Who are those wretched women sent up in the city van to the police-court, apprehended for drunkenness? They will be locked up in jail; but what will be done with the groggeries that made them drunk? Who are these men in the city-prison? That man stole a pair of shoes; that boy, one dollar from the counter; that girl snatched a purse—all villanies of less than twenty or thirty dollars' damage to the community; but for that gambler, who last night took that young man's thousand dollars—nothing! For that man who broke in upon the purity of a Christian household, and by a perfidy and adroitness that beat the strategy of hell, flung that girl into the chasm of earthly despair, from which her lost soul goes shrieking to the bottomless pit—nothing! For those who "fleeced" a young man, and induced him to filch from his employers vast sums of money, until, in his agony, he came to an officer of the church, and frantically asked what he should do—nothing!

Verily, small crimes ought to be punished; but it were more just if our authorities would turn out from our jails and penitentiaries the small villains, the petty criminals, the infantile offenders, the ten-dollar desperadoes, and fill their places with some of these monsters of abomination, who drive their roan span through our fine streets until honest men have to fly to escape being run over; and if they would turn out from their incarceration the poor girls of the town, and put in some of the magnificent ladies who cover up the sidewalk with their unpaid-for fineries, and with scornful look, in the church-aisle, pass the daughters of poverty, who with their faded dress and plain hat *dare* to come to worship God in the same sanctuary.

But all these wrongs shall be righted. Our streets shall hear the tramp of a regenerated multitude. Three hundred and sixty bells were rung in Moscow when the prince was married; but when righteousness and peace shall "kiss each other" in all the earth, ten thousand bells will strike the jubilee. Poverty enriched. Hunger fed. Disease cured. Crime purified. The cities saved.

THE END.